"No Change"

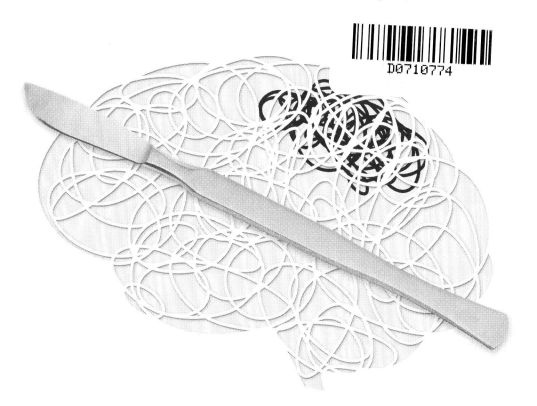

Living with Grade IV Glioblastoma Multiforme

by long-term survivor Mark Almas and caregiver wife Kim

A special thanks to my sister-in-law, Kristin Thompson, for helping me with Amazon and the digital print and on-line distribution process, and to Jason Demetri, rayrock.com, for your help building the website. Thank you both for helping me cross the finish line.

To order books, go to **Hope4GBM.com**

Dedication

This book is dedicated to my Uncle Mike Bahan.
You've been such an amazing support during this season in my life;
support that only one facing a similar disease,
with death imminent, can identify with.

My uncle is living proof there is Hope.

My wife Kim. You never gave up Hope. You misled me
to my face and I love you for it (lol). Seeing the look on
Dr Nelson's face and all in the room was worth it.
You have the courage of David with the gentleness of Ruth.
I love you so much.

To Max and Zac. I'm so sorry you had to grow up so fast.
Not being able to play with you like a normal dad, those times
that became known as awkward moments with dad …
I'm so very proud of the young men you've become.

There's Hope in front of all of us.

Foreword

When Mark asked me to write a foreword for his book I was honored that someone would think of me as they write about their life. I have thought long and hard about life, its meaning and purpose, and my responsibility in living it. In fact, these thoughts about life tend to dominate my mind as I log endless miles exploring our wonderful world on a motorcycle. Many have asked what a neurosurgeon is doing riding around on a motorcycle when so much of his life is spent repairing the brains and spines of those injured on such a contraption. The answer is simple in concept: The motorcycle opens my mind to the universe that grinds relentlessly on outside of me. Neurosurgery, probably like so many other fields, dominates every aspect of the lives of those who find themselves practicing it. Thousands of patients' lives and well being are constantly in the balance. We are endlessly fulfilling the requirements of hospitals, licensing agencies, the medical boards and battling to remain solvent in an ever increasingly complex medicolegal and reimbursement world. Superimposed on these worries are the concerns of life and family matters. It is comparable I would say to being a quarterback in a superbowl game that is played out every week. It seems that we are constantly addressing life and death more directly than virtually any other profession and yet, despite this, I am not so sure that neurosurgeons as a group find much time to contemplate the philosophical and spiritual point of it all. My window to reality is the motorcycle and on it I have spent the miles trying to resolve life's meaning just as a reader of Mark's book will be trying to resolve that for themselves. One of the apparent luxuries that I have, although it may be an illusion, is that I don't feel the constraint of time in my contemplation. When Mark was diagnosed with GBM 7 years ago perhaps the time constraint that science placed on him was an illusion as well?

Tonight I took my daughter out to see the crescent moon and Saturn and Jupiter preparing for their co-mingling on 12/21/20 in a few days. The universe grinds on. The moon, the planets, the stars, they are going to be here for thousands of more years. They dance around our solar system and galaxy and yet they are right there for all of us to behold. I'm showing them to my daughter while all around the world others are gazing up and simultaneously appreciating them. God gives them to all of us. He gave them to our great grandparents and our distant grandchildren. Someday they will take a moment to look up and see the beauty in the sky.

So much of the world is that way. It is here and it changes slowly over the eons and we get but a moment to appreciate it. A human life is but a mist that vanishes in the wind (James 4:14) compared to the timelessness of both God and the universe.

All of us, no matter what our station in life are on a journey walking down the same path together. We begin the same and we all end the same. Many of us spend our lives trying to fool ourselves about either our station, or our path or our destiny but this is no way to spend one's life. "Our lives are not a simple candle, but a splendid torch that we hold for but a moment and we make it burn as bright as possible before handing it on to future generations" (George Bernard Shaw). This book is precisely the torch that Mark is passing on to the generation that follows him. Through it we have a glimpse into his journey and the journey of both his wife and children. This should give us insight into our own. The contemplation, the questions, the realizations that Mark has experienced can be applied to our lives. Mark's story is one of emerging from the fog of illusion into reality and perhaps his rebirth will bring life and purpose to each of us as well?

E. Lee Nelson, MD with Mike Kiley, PA
Boulder Neurological and Spine Associates, January 2021

Contents

15   Day of doctors: a prologue

25   Background

45   "Wa wah, wa wah wah wah"

61   God is there all the time

75   Round two

89   Game time

105   Recovery

119   My wife

145   Therapy

159   Coming home

179   Making memories

203   Healthcare heroes

209   On another note

219   One of many opinions

231   Finishing day of doctors: Epilogue

241   Max's Story (By Max Almas)

261   Zac's Story (By Zac Almas)

275   Caregiving (By Kim Almas)

Here We Go Again...
Journal entry by Kim Almas   Aug 3, 2013

Hi Friends and Family,

I can't believe it's been two years since I updated our blog! This entry is going to be a little different from the last one (besides the fact that we switched to Caring Bridge) ...

After 4 years of clean mri's and thinking we were out of the woods, we got quite a shock with Mark's annual mri— Mark's cancer has returned. This tumor is about 1/3 the size of the previous, and appears to be a little more invasive. The neurosurgeon and the tumor board agreed that surgery is necessary, and recommended a more aggressive approach.

They have also recommended radiation following.

Surgery will be August 28, at 7:30 a.m. Please pray for the tumor to shrink or disappear before then; for the surgeon to have wisdom and success; and for the surgery to not further impair Mark's mobility or leave him with any other side effects. Please also pray for us to walk this well, to keep trusting the Lord, and to feel a profound peace.
Thank you!!

~Kim

PS ~~ If you want some background, the link to our previous blog is twoboysmom-standingontherock.blogspot.com

01

Day of doctors: a prologue

4:45 am, my alarm goes off. The last thing I want to do is get out of bed. A few minutes later I hear my wife bringing me a latte from our Tassimo coffee maker. I roll over, adjust my bed, and begin to drink my latte while I watch the morning headlines.

5:00 am, I pour myself out of bed to get ready for the day. Other than background noise from the TV, I'm in a fog. Brushing my teeth I notice all the hair I continue to leave in the sink every morning.

6:00 am, I head to our mud room to put on my braces and shoes. This process takes about 15 minutes, as I have a lot of weakness on my right side. Still in a fog, Kim joins me in the mud room to put her shoes on, and to let me know she's going to warm up the car.

6:20 am, I join Kim in the car to drive to University of Colorado, Anschutz Medical Campus, Aurora, CO – a suburb of Denver. After Kim offers up a short prayer, we begin our trip.

The sun is just beginning to smile as we leave our house for my "day of doctors." I can't remember if the radio was on – Kim likes to drive in silence – but I do remember the trip seemed normal, the small talk/silence you would expect. As we drive, the seams in the highway add to the repetition. I notice things like all the oil derricks, some pumping, others not, new fracking rigs being set up, and all the new construction near the Denver International Airport; all, I'm sure I've seen before, but today grab my interest. As we near the hospital, it seems once again we forget which lane we should be in to exit the highway. We laugh because it's the same conversation we have at this point every trip to the hospital.

As we pull into the parking lot we notice the hospital changed their parking process. The way they used to direct parking led to major congestion. With the changes made, we find ourselves early to my appointment. We sign in, sit in the waiting room, and wait for my name to be called.

"Mr. Almas?" the nurse calls. With a hug and kiss, I leave Kim in the waiting room. I'm taken to the changing room to get fitted with fashionable hospital attire – loose, with the drafty back-side. After donning my new fashion, I place all my personal belongings in a locker, then wait for my nurse to come back to get me. She walks me down to a room to get my IV inserted. This will be used to inject contrast during the final scans of the MRI. I never know how long this will take. I used to be an easy stick but lately, not-so-much. Following, my nurse helps me down the hall, around a corner, through double doors, to the room where the MRI equipment is.

Before entering the room I'm asked to hand over my cane, locker key, and eye glasses – as the MRI uses a very powerful magnet. Every time I'm given the third degree about my cartilage ear ring. They are concerned about it causing artifacts on the film, or that it may be ripped from my ear during the scan. They are still very reluctant after I assure them my Oncologist said she has never seen artifacts on the film and I've never felt even the slightest tug.

I'm assisted into the room and helped onto the table. A comfort pad is placed under my legs giving them support, along with a warm blanket. Earphones are placed in my ears – set to play 80s music – padding is placed on both sides of my face as they slide the head guard down over my head to keep it from moving during the procedure, and then I'm slid into the MRI tube.

In the tube, is the hardest time for me. This is 40 minutes that I can't escape reality. It seems even if I am able to rest my eyes, it is hard not thinking about what this test means. Unless God continues to prove my doctors wrong, this cancer will leave my wife a widow and my two boys without their dad.

Following my MRI, a technician and nurse help me off the table and back to the dressing room where I exchange my trend-setting fashion for my normal shorts attire. I meet up with Kim in the waiting room, then head to the cafeteria for a late breakfast, and wait.

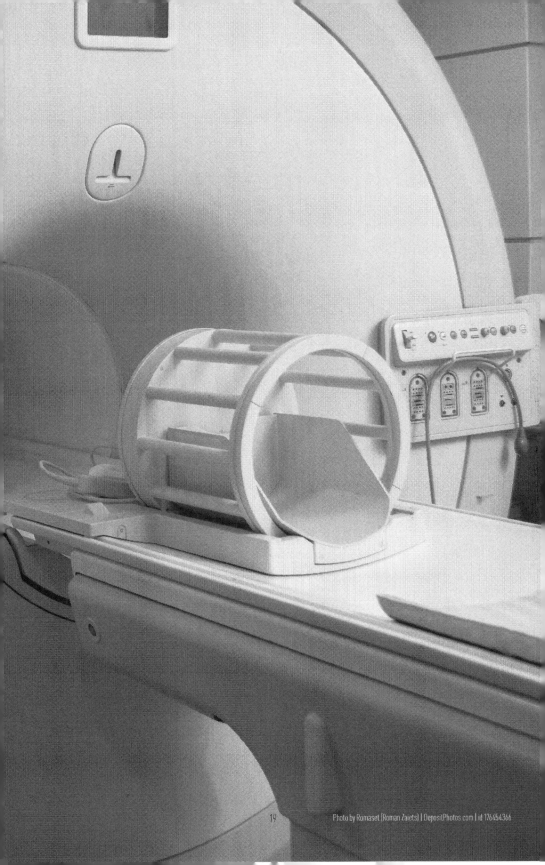

Let's start at the beginning . . .

Meeting with Neurosurgeon
Journal entry by Kim Almas   9/24/2009

We had our meeting today with the neurosurgeon, and feel confident with him. He said that the "brain mass" is "almost certainly at least a low grade tumor, level 2." Therefore, he recommends surgery to remove it and to do a biopsy.

We should know the exact surgery date by Monday, but it will most likely be around the end of October or beginning of November. Mark will be at a hospital in Boulder that has state-of-the-art mri technology, which will enable the surgeon to see mri images of his brain in "real time" as he works. (It's the only hospital in this 5-state region that has this equipment.) It will be a four-hour surgery, and he will be in the hospital anywhere from one to four days.

It was explained to us that almost all brain tumors are considered "malignant" on some level (which does not have the connotations it used to have). What that means is that Mark will very possibly need some chemotherapy and/or radiation after we hear the results of the biopsy. There is also a good possibility that he will need a second "follow-up" surgery to remove anything "missed" in the first surgery.

On an encouraging note, this neurosurgeon believes that there is a chance that the tumor is causing the problems in Mark's leg (unlike the opinion of the neurologist we first saw). So, hopefully that will be taken care of with the surgery.

When we find out the exact date of the surgery, I will post again on the blog.

We are feeling kind of drained, but overall are doing well.

Thank you again for all the kind and encouraging words, and especially for the prayer! It makes a difference!

Surgery Date
Journal entry by Mark Almas 9/28/09

I guess it is for real. I just got a call from the neurosurgeon and we have a date for surgery, October 7. I will be fitted for a fashionable hospital gown at 5:30 a.m., a last minute mri at 6:30 a.m. and into surgery at 7:30 a.m. The surgery will take around 4 hours.

This earlier date for surgery is not due to any turn of events. We were told end of October or beginning of November, as a best guess to the next available time. We knew they had asked for earlier rather than later, per our request, due to our health plan. Nobody guessed it would be this fast.

So here we are. Buckle up and put on your knee pads.

02

Background

I grew up in a very conservative Christian family. I don't want it to sound bad but my faith early on was not mine but inherited from my family. My mom was a Christian all her life, and my dad became a Christian while in the Army. He grew up in a family that most would refer to as "from the other side of the tracks." It was a tough upbringing, but made him who he is today – the man I love very much.

My dad was self employed; my mom worked hard as a stay at home mom, making sure each of her five kids were where we were supposed to be and when. Being involved with her kids was priority. I am the youngest by four years, with a span of eight years separating us all. When I was young, my dad would say each of his children were God-given. Of course getting older … "surprise."

Growing up I never wanted for much. I was taught early the meaning of a dollar. I worked for my dad's trucking company off-and-on through Jr High and High School for spending money. He wanted my focus – as with my brothers and sister – to be on school. He provided an old Ford truck, that each of us kids learned to drive and use during school. Because I was four years the younger, there was never a fight over its use.

Summers in high school, I also worked for my brother, a contractor who built high-end custom homes. I loved working with my hands, pounding nails, standing up walls; seeing a home come together. So, my plan was to graduate high school, skip college and work for my brother.

I attended a very small Christian school. So small that you could play every sport, participate in every event, most without trying out.

I graduated in a class of 18 students. My senior year I took my second year of journalism which included producing the yearbook. I was chosen to be editor. Our Josten's rep took an interest in me and challenged me to pursue graphic design. I brushed it off, told him I was going to work for my brother. He persisted. Finally, after many conversations, he posed a question, "What do you have to lose? If you go to school and don't like it, you can always quit and work for your brother." This made sense to me.

I'm glad he pushed me. I only wish I could remember his name. I would love for him to see what his encouragement did for me, and the life it has allowed me to live. He was one person, along with many others, who played a major role in my life. I joke with my brother now how I love my office. Heat in the winter, air conditioning in the summer. Ok, I'm a lightweight.

When asked if I attended college, the answer is yes. When added up all together, I've attended more than four years, but I do not have a degree. I spent a semester at Bob Jones University, just after high school. I chose this school because my family had attended. I returned home following my first semester for critical knee surgery – long story, in short – this was my first major life lesson.

My dad asked me if I would return the following semester, to complete a year away. I agreed, but did not follow though. I always felt this harmed our relationship.

Instead I attended a year at a Community College to knock off some General Ed classes. Then, because of all the fun I was hearing through my friends they were having at college, I joined them attending The Master's College in Newhall, CA. However, Master's did not have a Graphics Arts program. I had a lot of fun attending there, but knowing the expense, that my dad was paying for it, that it was on his "happy scale" of 2 for me, and it was not getting me where I needed, I dropped out.

Each time I changed locations or schools, I would look for jobs in the graphics field to learn different aspects in the industry. First, as a paste-up/production artist at a small graphics shop in Sacramento, CA; second, production/designer for a quick printer in Valencia, CA, and then on to a full design studio in Valencia, CA. I would later in life look back to see it was God placing me at each venue giving me the skills for the next season in my life.

One time such as this, I was returning to Master's College following summer break, and was looking for work. The job I previously had at a small quick printer was no longer available. I took a drive through the local business park and saw this big building. Knowing that Lithography had to do something with print, I pulled into the parking lot of Delta Lithograph. It was about 3pm when I walked in and asked the receptionist if they were hiring. She asked me what I was looking for, I told her, she got on her phone, she asked me to have a seat, and a few minutes later a short older man walked in, wearing a gray apron. He introduced himself as "Willie," then invited me to walk with him down a long hallway. We talked the entire way.

MENTOR I credit Willy Blumhoff (Blumhoff Design) for developing my love for graphic design and becoming the designer I am today.

His German accent was very strong. When the door to his office closed, he asked me maybe two more questions, then asked if I had time right then to work. I said yes. He rotated his body, picked up a stack of art boards, placed them on the artist desk I had been leaning on, and said, "Let's get going." You see, he had a huge deadline the next day for Neutrogena, and both his employees didn't show up for work. We walked out of the office the next morning very early. Walking to our cars he asked me what I wanted to be paid.

What I learned that night was Delta Lithograph was one facility among a family of six print companies (sister), located all around the USA, specializing in all aspects of print – all these facilities were owned by Bertelsmann Printing & Manufacturing Corporation, a large German company – with the idea no matter the project one of the six sisters could handle it. Delta specialized in book manufacturing. Willie Blumhoff (Blumhoff Design) rented space from Delta and Delta used Blumhoff Design as their in-house art department. This allowed me to learn design from Willie, then prepare film to print what I designed.

Working with Willie, he encouraged me to attend Art Center School of Design of California. This was a school, I thought, way out of my league. You are accepted based on your portfolio. I didn't have one.

Willie taught design at the school prior and was able to get me into the night program. The next couple of years I worked full time during the day, then drove about an hour each way to Pasadena, CA, to attend a 2-4 hour class. Averaging four hours of sleep each night, not a fan of debt, and the fact I already had a position in a design studio (one of the hardest things to get out of school), I chose to stop.

Art Center was amazing. It was a time I didn't deserve but was fortunate to experience. I learned how to design for a global marketplace. I give credit to my understanding of design to a little, young-at-heart German man wearing a gray apron, who took an interest in me.

I've been a graphic designer now for over 30 years, much of that time in California, working for myself. I've worked with teams, with players, the best in the world talent, literally. I don't say this to brag; in fact, just the opposite. Every connection, client, award, opportunity I had, I consider given to me by God. It had to be. I don't have the degree. The talent debatable. Connections to get me where I have gotten? With every opportunity God provided me, He also provided me the creativity to meet the challenge and excel.

While professionally I am a graphic designer, I served my church in a volunteer role as their Programming Director. Working in this position, I worked with the Lead Pastor, Worship pastor, and other lay leaders, to design Sunday services and special events.

I had a great time doing this. I got to work with a great group of creative people, all volunteer, focused on bringing people into a personal relationship with Jesus Christ. We used music, video, drama, among other elements to support the spoken message.

Our team designed services to help guide people through national tragedies like September 11, 2001. We designed numerous Easter and Christmas services, all communicating the same seasonal message, but in fresh, new ways. We had a lot of fun throughout the year finding creative ways to help support our teaching pastor land the nugget of truth he wanted our guests to leave with – and we had fun – I had too much fun.

I was sensing God leading me to full-time ministry. The next couple of years I traveled the country looking at churches, some for ideas, others on interviews, and attend art conferences. Through this process, a very wise, older man (Dave Marty) in our small group, kept my wife and I in check. He knew my heart and passion could easily mislead me. I remember the first church that offered me a position was in a very small town in Ohio. I was so excited.

After I got home, I could not wait to see Dave. He listened to Kim and me tell about our trip. He was excited for us. When we were done talking, he said, "Let me ask you a question. Before you left, you said if this position had these three things, you would know God is in you taking it." It took us a half a second to realize we could not accept this position. The hardest phone call I made was to that pastor to let him know I would not be coming. I thank God for Dave and his spiritual counsel.

I had other offers but for one reason or another, we did not see it as a good fit. Driving home after a staff meeting one day, I was so discouraged. I thought ministry was my next season in life. As I drove, I was looking out the front windows of my car. I was on Highway 50 driving from El Dorado Hills, almost to Folsom, CA, when I started to laugh. Here I live in the "Golden State" and it was an ugly brown. A week earlier everything was green and beautiful. It only takes a couple of days in mid-April to change the open fields from deep green to an ugly brown. I wondered who was the marketing company who got credit for redefining brown to "golden." It just made me laugh.

A few days later I received a call from a church in Lafayette, CO. I'm still not sure how they heard about me. A couple weeks later, I was flying to Colorado for a face-to-face interview. Walking by myself into the empty auditorium, I remember sitting in one of the chairs in the back, calling Kim to say, "I believe we found our home." I had not even had a single formal interview, but I knew God called me to Flatirons Community Church. After a season of being discouraged, a cool God-thing for me was to formally accept a position at Flatirons Community Church, and on my birthday, 2004. About 2 months later we were moving to Colorado.

After watching the moving trucks leave, we spent the next week living with my parents, saying our "goodbyes" to our friends and family. October 1, 2004, the next season for our family began. Kim and Max, age 4, got into our Toyota van. I got into our BMW with Zac, age 2, and we headed for Colorado.

Kim is a pastor's daughter, so she knows about big life changes and moving around the country. Other than for college, I never lived out of California. Here we were moving to a state we loved to vacation in and dreamed to live in "someday," but here we were doing it. We were moving to a place we knew nobody, other than those we had briefly met on staff, during the interview process.

My emotions were mixed as we crossed the California border.
I remember being so excited to begin this new season/adventure,
of my family … When I saw the sign "Welcome to Nevada" tears
started to flow.

What drew me to Flatirons CC was they were a community of
real people reaching into the gutter to reach the lost for Christ.
A lot of churches say they do this, but in reality don't come close.
Not to criticize but it takes a special team of people to reach out
to a truly lost and broken world. While on staff, I heard, saw,
and experienced true life transformation.

One was a man who just started to attend Flatirons. He told us
in his search for truth he would look for churches with the word
"grace" in its name. He visited three churches, each in which he
was made very unwelcome. One pastor actually told him he'd rather
he not come back. He was afraid he would cause the men in his
church to stumble. You see, he was gay. This devastated him.
The last church he was so discouraged he almost succeeded in
taking his life. While in a coma, he said he saw the persona of
Christ telling him to continue his search. Shortly after getting out
of the hospital, he was having breakfast with a friend talking about
finding a church. The waitress overheard their conversation and

suggested he try Flatirons, just down the street. He said from the moment he entered the building, he felt acceptance. He met God and shortly after gave himself to Christ.

God transformed this man before my eyes in every way. He was so excited about what God was doing in his life, giving him the strength to conquer his addictions. When he got baptized, I had the pleasure to be on camera filming the lane he was in. We were baptizing over 300 people, so we set up 4 lanes with a camera capturing each lane. Without knowing, he was in my lane. I was so happy. He had such a hard life and to see that he was now anchored firmly to Biblical truths was amazing.

In Colorado it is not uncommon for a lake to lose oxygen, and of course when that happens all the fish die. The lake we used for baptisms lost its oxygen the week before. Many staff and volunteers were there on a daily basis cleaning it of dead fish. Randy Travis has a song "Pray For The Fish." He wrote it about his baptism. Wouldn't you know that when this man was coming up out of the water, in the top-left-corner of the screen floats a dead fish. I started chuckling. The camera was bouncing a bit, but I was so excited that he found a safe spiritual home to learn that God accepts messy people. Before he passed away from a heart attack, I witnessed true transformation, a God transformation. I look forward to seeing him again in heaven.

Another was overhearing a conversation between the High Priestess of the Satanic Church and my pastor following a service. She said she had attended a couple weekend programs but wasn't sure she should be there. She said when she's in attendance, she feels unconditional love. I knew I was serving at the right church when my pastor responded, "This is exactly where you need to be." Where else would she meet Jesus?

I was on staff at Flatirons for about three years. I enjoyed my experience very much. I loved working with a creative team with an eternal focus. I knew my time was coming to an end when the smallest of things would bug me. Of course with a new lead pastor (boss) comes change; not that change is bad, sometimes it's just change. Very few of the people remained on the creative team as when I arrived. I couldn't figure out why this change was happening? God called me to ministry. My heart was into making ministry work. It took me about six months to realize my time at Flatirons was done, and time to move on to my next season.

Once believing God was leading me to a career in full-time ministry,
I now realized God was using me along with a bunch of other
creative people, most from the secular world, to help transition
Flatirons from one pastor to the next. Flatirons is a very high-energy
environment. During a transition of lead pastors, churches tend to
decrease in size. Not only did Flatirons not decrease, it grew.
I believe God used my creativity along with all the other members
on the "Attract Team" to make this happen.

After turning in my resignation, and walking back to my office,
I remember thinking, "What next?" While at Flatirons I worked very
long hours; that was where my heart was. I did not have time
to do much freelance work. Because Colorado was still a fairly
new place for me to live, I really had no business connections.
I had done a little work for a friend of mine but not much.
When I got back to my office I picked up the phone to call my friend
and business associate, Rabs Hughey. He let me know earlier that
morning in their team meeting, the conversation came up about
recruiting me. We met later that day for coffee. I walked out of that
meeting with a contract that would take about 40% of my time,
but would more than cover my monthly needs. I say this to affirm
the promise that God gives us, He will take care of our needs.
We had no idea how even more important this would be.

Background

Heading to Boulder Community Hospital this morning was surreal. Getting prepped for brain surgery... really? Is this going to hurt?

Surgery Update #1
Journal entry by Kim Almas   10/7/09

Just heard from one of our nurses. Everything is going well. Actual surgery began around 9:15 (lots of prep work before the actual surgery I guess).

He was in a good state of mind (haha) before he went in, and the rest of us are doing fine too.

God is good, all the time :)

Thanks for the continued prayer!

Surgery Update #2
Journal entry by Kim Almas   10/7/09

Surgery took a little longer, but just because
you never quite know what you'll get once you
get in there.

They did a final mri to make sure they
"got" all they could. Now they're doing
the final steps to take him from surgery to
recovery.

We'll talk to the surgeon in a few minutes,
and I'll put up the next update after that.à

Surgery Update #3
Journal entry by Kim Almas   10/7/09

Surgery went well! Going to see him in
icu shortly.

On to Rehab
Journal entry by Kim Almas 10/10/09

They finally transferred Mark out of icu
and up to Rehab on the fourth floor. (He had
been able to move from icu sooner, but there just
weren't any beds available.)

Technically, he could even go home at
this point, but because his leg is so weak,
he decided to opt for some therapy that our
insurance provides for. How long he'll be
here all depends on how quickly he improves,
but it will be anywhere from three to ten days.

The boys finally got to see him today too!
That was good, very very good (for all of us)
:-)

If you're in the area, come on in and say hi, if you'd like. I know he'd like that :-) Just give us a heads-up if you do, though, so we can make sure he's not in the middle of therapy (which will be at least three hours a day, spread throughout the day).

Many thanks again for all the encouraging notes! I was able to read several to him today that he hadn't seen yet, and he was really overwhelmed...

The wi-fi isn't as good up here, so that may slow down communication a bit. I'll check email and the blog when I can.

03

"Wa wah, wa wah wah wah"

Just before leaving the staff at Flatirons in 2007, I was on our Attract Team's Creative Retreat staying at a church member's mountain house. During the night I woke up and could not feel or move my right leg. I thought I had slept wrong and it was just asleep. No matter what I did I could not "wake it up." Also, during the night, it started snowing, hard. Concerned we would get snowed in, we decided to cut our retreat short to head back home. Riding home

I made an appointment with my chiropractor. He diagnosed that during the night my sacroiliac – a word until then I thought was a cartoon word – opened up and closed pinching my sciatic nerve. He said depending on the length of time the nerve was pinched, that would determine the amount of damage to my sciatic nerve. I began to see him on a daily basis, then every other day, then twice a week, then once a week, then once a month; you get the picture.

About the same time I started to have "localized seizures" in my right leg. I alerted my general practitioner and we both assumed it was just damage from the pinched nerve. But to be safe he sent me to a neurologist. He did all kinds of tests, but nothing showed up. After about a year and a half (in 2009), I was at an appointment with my general practitioner for an unrelated issue, and trying to save a buck I asked him, "What's next? I'm afraid I've got MS." What I didn't know was this was the key word to get an MRI of my brain.

I received a call from my doctor a couple days later. My office was located above my garage in our carriage house. He left a voice mail letting me know something showed up on the MRI. Now if I could describe him I would say he is David Letterman with M.D. after his name – a very funny guy. His tone left me at ease, but with urgency to follow up with my neurologist, immediately.

It was around 9am when I got in touch with my neurologist. At first
he seemed puzzled why I had an MRI taken. With the information my
doctor and I had given him, he was focusing on the leg not my brain.
The conversation quickly changed to "can you come see me today."
As he looked for a time to fit me in, I soon realized this was not
a normal call. He had no free time other than over his lunch hour.
That was my first sign that things were not good.

After finding a place for our boys to stay, we headed up to
Longmont, CO, to meet with my neurologist. He asked if we had
seen the MRI? We told him no, and he invited us down the hall
to a room where he began to show us what the MRI revealed.
As he clicked through each layer going down through my brain
he said, "This is where it starts." As he continued to click through
the layers, I felt like I was getting lost in a "Peanuts" cartoon.
All I could hear was "wa wah, wa wah wah wah." Knowing Kim is
the astute one in the family, I was relying on her to pick up on
what he was laying down. What I didn't realize, the same "Peanuts"
cartoon was playing in her head.

After the shock of seeing my MRI, we spent time with my neurologist.
He reviewed what we just saw and began to explain what we should
expect next. He gave us a few names of surgeons so we could begin

our research. He said that pending the neurosurgeon's opinion, they may want to do a biopsy first. I'm so glad Kim checked in, because I was still in the "Peanuts" episode, and not the one with Snoopy dancing.

Driving home was quiet. We both were thinking about what just happened. It was probably halfway home when I broke the quiet by asking Kim, "Exactly how do they get a biopsy from your brain?" I knew the term. I thought I knew what it was. Hearing that a surgeon would be drilling holes in my head – crazy.

After getting home my first call was to my dad. I didn't know but he was helping my oldest brother, Mike, drive home a truck for his trucking company. I gave my dad a brief overview of my doctor visit and the results of the MRI. He asked if I wanted to talk, which of course I said yes … It was then I broke, realizing the impact this could have on my family's future. They both wanted to backtrack and come see me. I assured them I was emotionally OK, and with what I heard earlier, I was pretty sure I would see them soon.

Later that day, I called Rabs. Since he was the middle-man for my largest client, I felt I needed to bring him up to speed as soon as possible. We met at a coffee shop a couple days later and

I gave him the news. After a very long pause: Rabs: What side of your brain is it on? Me: (Thinking) What the … huh … ? Rabs: What side of your brain is it on? I realized he was asking me if this would affect my creativity. This was his way to deal with a serious situation. After we got done laughing, he asked me, "Do you believe God is sovereign, or not?" Of course I did, and I was at peacc.

I let Rabs know that in about three weeks I had an appointment with a surgeon and I would have more information then. We talked a little business, then agreed to talk retainer after I met with the neurosurgeon.

My neurologist provided the name of a great neurosurgeon. We felt very comfortable with Ewell Lee Nelson, MD. He spoke very directly, which sometimes was very unsettling but was reality. When we checked on his degrees/accreditations, he always came out on top or was teaching the new method. He recommended that I have my surgery at Boulder Community Hospital. He said they were one of three hospitals in the country, at that time, to have real-time MRI. This machine allows surgeons to see, in real-time, what they are doing during surgery. I didn't know that without this equipment it was common to need multiple surgeries due to the delicate nature.

We believe without doubt that God provided him to us.

After meeting with Dr. Nelson I called Rabs. I knew he was in Austin, TX, at a team meeting – no answer. He returned my call later that night when he was at the airport prior to boarding his flight home. I brought him up to speed with a tentative schedule. As I transitioned the conversation to retainer, he cut me off. He told me earlier that day in their team meeting, they prayed for me. They decided no matter what, they would take care of me and my family, and for me to continue sending my monthly invoices.

Total God thing.

About a month later, my alarm went off at 4:50am. I didn't need to set the alarm – I didn't sleep. Sign-in was at 7am – tons of paperwork – immediately followed with getting fitted with hospital attire – then more paperwork. After getting all the IVs inserted, nurses shaved squares in my hair where they would attach the diodes that would be used to sync the position of my head with the real-time MRI – more questions and paperwork. Feeling like an electronic checkerboard, I got wheeled down the hall for my last MRI just before surgery. Getting back to my room, I found Kim talking with the nurses, and yes, filling out more paperwork.

Remember that real-time MRI I was telling you about? As I'm lying on the gurney, Dr. Nelson came in to read me all the legal jargon before surgery. Everything from paralyzing me to killing me. He also informed me that the machine that he talked up so much broke down a lot, in that very matter-of-fact tone – the same tone we had grown accustomed to. I remember saying, "And you're telling me this now, why?" A nurse behind him gave me a big thumbs up while laughing. I'm sure his bedside manner is due to the seriousness of the surgeries he performs.

The surgery lasted six hours followed by time in recovery. It is there where they start to determine what types of therapy I will need – quality of life. Kim was very concerned when the therapist in recovery asked me what color the sky was and with full confidence I answered green. When asked a second time, I repeated green. Kim jokingly says she was thinking, "Oh my gosh, my husband's a vegetable." Things like walking, talking, eating – things I took for granted – I now had to relearn.

They removed a tumor about the size of a golf ball, considered to be a Grade 2 Astrocytoma. For the most part, considered benign.

I was assigned speech therapy for thought processing, physical therapy for lower body movement, and occupational therapy for upper body movement. Each session would last about 30 minutes, with a break in between each. It may not sound like much, but it would wipe me out. I found value with each PT and OT session. Speech was very frustrating, and became the battle of the minds, literally. We would play all kinds of games to demonstrate how I think; games likes Sudoku or Rush Hour (the game where you move plastic cars and trucks around trying to get a specific car across the board). If I did not play the games how she wanted, I was incorrect and I was marked down. Even before surgery I played these games differently than she did. She got upset because I kept beating her. It didn't matter if I could do it in fewer moves, or was just plain faster, she took it personally, and would mark me down.

Occupational and physical therapy were very helpful. Both would completely exhaust me. After each 30 minute session, I would go back to my room and sleep. At the beginning, I would need to be woken up to attend my next session. Later a nap would suffice.

Every session targeted quality-of-life. The therapists were trying to reroute "circuitry" in my brain, to perform the daily tasks I was able to do before surgery, but with a chunk of my brain missing. For instance, when you're eating and want a drink, how do you pick up your glass without running your hand or arm through the mashed potatoes? I saw the mashed potatoes. I knew the mashed potatoes were there. But, I would still run my hand and arm through them on the way to pick up my drink. I don't know how many times I did this. On a side note, I am happy to report that today I no longer run my hand through my mashed potatoes or any other food on my plate to pick up my drink.

Visitors were great, I had a lot. Rabs and Erik were the best. These are two men that I worked with in Austin, TX, and both gave me a bad time about my "spiky, artsy hairstyle." I returned the banter by making comments about them being hair impaired. Both shaved their heads, for different reasons. They walked in the door expecting to see me with no hair. To their surprise I had so much hair, it was hard to find where the surgeon cut. Almost in unison they said, "Oh crap!" They couldn't get over the fact that my head was not shaved. They did spend time hunting for the 63 staples.

I had to learn to walk all over again. I remember my mom during one session, at the end of the hallway, arms out, as if she was waiting for her toddler to walk for the first time. For me, it was frustrating. I knew how to walk. My brain just wasn't processing to my arms or legs what to do. With a lot of therapy, and the amazing therapists, I was able to leave the hospital walking with the use of a brace for drop-foot and a cane.

After I was released I was required to continue my therapy sessions on an outpatient basis, even speech. I thought speech was a waste of time but I was excited that I would be able to get the other extended therapy. I was told I would receive occupational and physical therapy at one location, and speech at another location. I was told I would hear from therapy within the next couple days to schedule.

Arriving back home was the best. When we pulled up to the house, there was a big banner that my two boys made me (age 9 and 7), along with help from their Nana and Grandma, hanging from our front porch railing, saying "Welcome Home Dad!"

The first few days home, I enjoyed time with my boys and resting. Max and Zac were very careful with me. I loved being home.

A WONDERFUL SIGHT Arriving home I'm greeted by this amazing banner created by Max (9) and Zac (7) along with a little help by both grandmas.

Outpatient appointments were being set up. Now remember my experience with the speech therapist at the hospital?

When outpatient called, the conversation went like this:

Therapist: Hello, may I speak with a Mr. Mark Almas?

Me: This is he.

Therapist: I mean the Mark Almas that just had brain surgery?

Me: This is he.

MY FAMILY Max, Me, Zac and Kim – Shirts custom made by our brother-in-law's brother.

Therapist: (Long pause, very puzzled) I need to set up a therapy session for you, for speech. Were you were aware of this?

Me: Yes.

Therapist: Do you know why they're asking you to go through more speech therapy?

Me: Not really. I think it's because I butted heads with my therapist.

Therapist: Who was your therapist?

Me: I told her the therapist's name.

Therapist: Ooooh .....Gotcha.

Therapist: Can you come see me tomorrow at 2:30?
Shouldn't take long, but I do need to ask you a few things
to sign you off.

Me: Absolutely, goodbye.

After about a 5-minute meeting, I was signed off for speech
therapy.

Home

Journal entry by Kim Almas   10/16/09

Mark is home! :-) We are so happy :-)
He is doing really well.

The boys made big "Welcome Home, Dad"
posters, which Nana hung on the porch
railing for him to see as we drove up :-)

Next week we start up with all sorts of
appointments, but for the next few days we rest.

Baby Steps and Legos (Note from Mark)

I just wanted to thank all of you who have
been praying and loving on my family
during this season of our life. Some of you
I may never know but I will remember by the

peace you helped provide me through your prayer, confirming God is in control and we have an awesome God!

Today I got to go home. Yeah!

Now I look forward to playing Legos with my boys. They are going to enjoy playing with dad. Who knew it would be the simple things like this that will help reprogram my brain and rehabilitate me back to a full recovery.

I have a lot to relearn, and so much to be thankful for. With baby steps and Legos I am on a path to a full recovery!

In His grip!

m

04

God is there all the time

The next couple years, I learned how to do life but just a little differently. Having severe drop foot, I needed a brace to lift my toes up from the floor and a cane to walk. Some things were more difficult to do than others – like getting in and out of a car, and steps.

A couple years prior, experiencing those localized seizures in my right leg, I started driving with my left foot. So, driving was not that big a deal. I was able to visit with clients and keep a full schedule. Soon I was traveling for work again, mainly to Austin, TX, and Atlanta, GA, with sporadic trips to San Fransisco and Los Angeles.

I love snowboarding. One day, talking to my neighbor John, he said he had a friend that worked with the adaptive ski program at a local hill. He scheduled a day for us to go skiing. We met his friend early in the morning and after signing a bunch of paperwork, getting sized for equipment, and him asking me some questions, we headed to the slopes. Even though they were skis, it was so good to feel the snow again.

He took me over to this little bump and asked me to put on my skis. Then he showed me some things to test my balance and then he asked me to ski down the bump. I fell. I got up, got my balance, skied a little forward, and fell. This happened a few more times before I got down to the bottom of the bump. This happened a few more times before I got down the entire bump without falling.

My instructor thought it was time for a "bunny hill," the most basic of hills, used for beginners. I felt pretty good. We all got in the chairlift line. On our turn, the chair came swinging around and I sat down – success. Then thoughts of offloading came into my mind – that's where most "garage sales" happen. I'm happy to say I exited the lift without crashing. A little wobbly but I didn't crash. After each run I felt more stable than the one before. It felt so good back on the mountain – the sounds, the smells, and the snow.

Following lunch I asked my instructor if I could try to snowboard. So we switched skis for a board and headed back to the bump.

This proved to be more difficult because of my balance issue. I would stand up and fall on my butt. Over and over I tried. I really wanted to snowboard with my two boys. Before I gave up, I asked my instructor if I could get a couple ski poles. A few tries later, I was up and snowboarding – no snowboarder wants to get caught skiing. I'm sure I was not in style using ski poles, but I was snowboarding, and ready for my boys.

John taught me so much more than how to snowboard that day, but how to receive a blessing. Not long after that, we hit the slopes as a family for the first time.

We continued making memories exploring the beauty Colorado has to offer, while I gained strength. At one doctor visit, I asked my doctor how long before I could say I was cured. He told me that the old thought was that in five years if the cancer did not return you

BLESSINGS First time on the slopes as a family, post first surgery.

were considered cancer free, but they have come to realize that if the cancer didn't come back in a year, pretty much, you're cured. He showed me a bell curve where he said, "At surgery you really piss off the cancer, but if the cancer doesn't come back within the first year, things are looking pretty good." It seemed odd from what I had believed, but I took it as very good news.

With that information, a couples years after surgery, Kim and I wanted to turn the page in this season of our family's life. Max and Zac were only 9 and 7 when I was diagnosed. We wanted to do something special, something big, something we'd never done before – for them. Kim found a Disney Cruise, the inaugural cruise of Disney's ship Fantasy – its fourth cruise.

Our itinerary took us to Grand Cayman, where we stayed on the ship and played; Costa Maya, where we hiked over and around Mayan ruins; Cozumel, where we swam with dolphins; and Castaway Cay (Disney's private island), where we played more. This was what we all needed.

Boarding the ship we were totally blown away. In true Disney fashion we were welcomed aboard, met some of the crew, had photos taken with a few cast members – they were all over the ship – invited to have lunch on the top deck for a buffet lunch while our luggage was taken to our room.

After lunch we explored the ship, and signed the boys into their respective clubs. We saw these really cool pictures on the wall that would come alive when you held your key card in front of them. Around 4pm, people began gathering for the deck party just before departure. When we noticed we were moving we worked our way to the front of the ship. Just as we got to open water, we noticed dolphins leading us out to sea. I thought, man, Disney thinks of everything – just joking – but it was so cool. I was confident this was the trip I was hoping for Max and Zac to turn the page.

When we got to dinner, we were seated with a family of four from the Philippines – two boys, same ages as ours. They introduced themselves, Paul and Karen Francia. After the normal introductions, we found out Paul was a neurosurgeon and Karen, an eye surgeon. Seeing how I was using a cane, Karen asked me my story. When I told her I had brain cancer, she asked who my neurosurgeon was and where I had my surgery. I told her Dr. Lee Nelson, Boulder Community Hospital. She smiled and said that Paul had attended a conference where my surgeon was the keynote speaker the previous year. Karen leaned over to me and said, "You didn't know you were operated on by the best, did you?" When we picked Dr. Nelson, we knew he was extremely qualified, but this was affirmation that God directed us to the best. Here we were on a Caribbean cruise, full of mostly Americans, sitting at a table with a neurosurgeon from the Philippines testifying to the skill of my surgeon, giving power to God's faithfulness.

Each evening we would see each other at dinner, talk about our day, the excursions we took, cool things we saw on the ship – shows or movies we saw … the week was amazing.

But, in true Disney fashion, it was not over. The second to the last night, after a full day at sea, we had a deck party,

LEFT TO RIGHT Kim Almas, Max Almas, Alex Francia, Paul Francia, Disney Cast Members Dennis and Em, David Francia, Karen Francia, Zac Almas and Mark Almas (me).

"Pirates in the Caribbean," This was a production using the outside deck screens, onstage production, theatrics, and "first time ever, from a ship" fireworks show. I remember watching Zac, standing on a large stage box, looking up into a dark Caribbean sky, watching the fireworks. He looked so happy and at peace. I had not seen this in a long time. This was a very good day.

Before we got off the ship, we had breakfast with the Francias and said our goodbyes. We remain in contact today.

Not Alone!
Journal entry by Kim Almas 8/22/13

It's a crazy thing, this waiting time before a major, possibly life-changing surgery.

We suddenly see every little job that "must" get done "now," although maybe that's just a subconscious effort to stay distracted with busyness.

We have ups, and we have downs ~ sometimes all within the space of 5 min.

We try to plan and think ahead, and then we realize we can only do so much with the information we have right now.

We try to research treatment options one minute (and have to Google for every-other-ginormous-word we read), and can't figure out what to make for dinner the next minute.

We are exhausted, and yet can't sleep.

We feel anxious, and yet we trust.

Our heads sometimes spin.

And then, in the middle of all of the craziness, we receive reminders, seemingly out of the blue, that we are not in this alone.

* Encouraging notes via text, email, Facebook, Caring Bridge, and even snail mail.

* Offers of help.

* Kind words.

*Prayers from people we don't even know.

*Freezer meals and meal sign-ups.

*Scripture verses sent our way.

*Hugs and lots of, "We're praying!" reminders.

And more . . .

Every single thing means so much, and has helped us immensely in our goal to stay positive!

Philippians 4 has some encouragement and promises that we're finding to be perfect for right now.

In verse 6, we're reminded to not be anxious, but pray with a thankful heart.

In verse 7, we have the promise that comes with that reminder ~~ "peace that passes understanding," because of that prayer. (We have found this to be true!)

Verse 8 reminds us to keep focused on things that are good (well, lots of other words there, but that's the idea).

(Our God is good, and we trust Him!

And finally, verse 13 reminds us that we can do all things, through Christ who gives us strength. That includes getting through this chapter in our lives!

Thank you, friends, for your love and kindness, and for helping us head into this, in such meaningful, truly helpful, and thoughtful ways.

We are grateful, and we are blessed, and we love you!

~Kim

Frontal Lobe

– Thinking

– Speaking

– Reasoning

– Problem Solving

Parietal Lobe

– Reading

– Body Orientation

– Sensory Information

– Understanding Language

Temporal Lobe

– Memories

– Hearing

– Behavior

– Generation Emotions

Occipital Lobe

– Vision

Cerebellum

– Coordination

– Balance

– Vestibular

– Attention

Brain Stem

– Breathing

– Temperature

– Heart Rate

05

Round two

2013 came, four years since my first surgery. The biggest change to me was the frequency of my MRI's. They had been every three to four months until 2011. Two in 2012 – six months apart and my final one in 2013.

A few days after my 2013 MRI, I was watching my boys' Tae Kwon Do workout when my iPhone rang. When I looked down Dr. Nelson's face was filling my iPhone screen. Because this was after hours

DISTRACTION Started boys in Tae-kwon-do after first diagnosis, celebrated both of them earning their black belts after 2nd surgery.

I knew this could not be good. I quickly walked outside while answering his call. He said the MRI showed something small but felt he needed to take it before the tumor board. He was pretty sure they would recommend surgery to be safe. I was stunned.

I sat in my car for what seemed like hours but was only minutes before I called my dad in California. He asked me if I needed him to fly out. Part of me wanted to say "yes" but since I was going to see him in about a week at my niece's wedding, I told him no. It was almost an out of body experience. He made sure I knew he was there for me. I was just numb.

I was still talking to my dad when Max and Zac finished their workout. Catching on, my dad quickly let me end the call, not to let the boys know what was going on. Driving home I was in and out of their conversation – I was driving home under the influence of being numb.

This was happening just a couple days before we left for a family vacation/wedding, that included a whirlwind 3-day visit to Washington D.C., my niece's wedding and Gettysburg in Pennsylvania, and a visit to the Creation Museum in Kentucky "just because we were in the neighborhood"…

When I got home, Kim already had dinner made and on the table. I tried to keep everything as normal as possible as we sat down to eat. I was glad Kim controlled the conversation during dinner, because I hadn't checked back in following my call with Dr. Nelson. After dinner the boys ran across the street to play with their friends at the park. I ask Kim to join me on the couch where I broke the news to her – we sat there and cried.

We decided to keep it under wraps until we had confirmation from Dr. Nelson and the tumor board; only my father was in the know. We also didn't want to cast a dark cloud over my niece's wedding. I arranged a time with Dr. Nelson to speak with him at a specific

time on Tuesday knowing that we would be in Washington, D.C.
We had fun being tourists, just concentrating on where we were at,
what we were seeing, the history, and the excitement we were
seeing in Max and Zac, while visiting our nation's historical landmarks.

With all the business travel I'd racked up, I accumulated a lot of
hotel points. We found ourselves having the privilege of staying at
the JW Marriott right on Pennsylvania Avenue – a couple blocks
from the White House. On Tuesday, before calling Dr. Nelson, we took
advantage of our hotel indoor swimming pool. Before jumping in,
I placed my iPhone, towel and t-shirt on a lounge chair near the pool.
We were having a lot of fun. Playing with Max and Zac – something
just didn't feel right. I felt my swimming trunks pocket and realized
my key card was not there but my iPhone was. Making light
of the situation, I pulled out my iPhone and asked Max and Zac
if they wanted to order pizza.

I was so sick to my stomach knowing all the images I took that day
were lost. Remember that "being cheap" thing? That came to bite
me in the butt that night. I didn't want to pay $50 bucks per day
for Internet service at the JW Marriott which would've allowed my
photos to automatically upload to the cloud. FYI, rice does not fix it.

Later that night, after getting back to our room, I went into the bathroom, stuffed towels under the door and called Dr Nelson (from Kim's phone). He said the tumor board did recommend surgery, and that his scheduler would contact me.

We continued to explore Washington, D.C, then drove to Kim's Aunt Marilyn and Uncle Dick's house in Pennsylvania, to visit and stay with while we attended my niece's wedding. They knew the cloud Kim and I were under, and provided such spiritual support. This was a visit set up months prior, not imagining what we were about to find out. To be in such a strong Christian family, for such a time as this, was a God thing.

DISTRACTION With Aunt Marilyn and Uncle Dick at Sight and Sound in Pennsylvania

Jenae's wedding was beautiful, but emotionally tough. The only person in attendance that knew what we were about to face was my dad, and we had been out of contact since my conversation with Dr. Nelson. When we arrived at the wedding, we were a little early. I saw my dad and brought him up to speed – told him not to tell anybody – this was Jenae's day and we wanted to help keep the atmosphere happy.

Soon after we returned home, we received our surgery date. Now we had to break the news to our boys. Until now they were unaware that my cancer had come back. When we told them, as you can imagine, they broke down. Max screamed out, "Why is God doing this to us? I can't do this!" This scared me. Through this challenge, we hoped it would grow the faith of Max and Zac. This was not what I had expected. (See their stories at the end.)

During this window, we had tremendous support from Kim's parents, from her cousins Mark and Sydney, and friends Craig and Anna. A couple weeks later, the week before surgery, I was asked to make a quick business trip to Austin, TX. I worked with my team a little bit before unexpectedly taking off with the creative lead team, to spend the afternoon on Erik's boat. This was so fun – relaxing, laughing, reminiscing – I had done life with some of these guys around seven years.

As evening came, Erik stopped the boat and turned the engine off. "So Mark," Erik said, "what are your plans?" I let them know that the only for sure I knew at that time was that the cancer would be at least a Grade 2, as it does not regress. If it was a Grade 2, I would most likely need some therapy. Pending how much more of the brain they cut out would determine what therapy I would need. I told them Grade 2 is not looked at as a life shortening form of cancer, so following surgery and therapy I would be back, but maybe doing life a bit differently.

I went on, Grade 3 is where they begin to consider this cancer to be life shortening, Grade 4 is a death sentence; and if I was diagnosed Grade 4, I'm out of here. I'm gonna take a long cruise, spend time with my family…all in jest, as I had no idea what was about to unfold. Then, as a team, we prayed.

This was an amazing time for me. Thank you, Erik, for arranging this. Just before major surgery, being able to spend a very fun day, with a group of guys whom I consider more my brothers than men I work with, wrapping up in a time in prayer – I was at peace.

Here we go!
Journal entry by Kim Almas 8/28/2013

Well, he's off! He has a great team
around him, not to mention all the prayer :-)
We are all tired but in good spirits, and are
expecting good things today! I will post
updates when I can.

Thank you for all the encouraging words,
and for continuing to pray!

Out of surgery

Journal entry by Kim Almas   8/28/2013

Mark is out of surgery, and we're waiting to see him. I'll update more when I can.

Untitled
Journal entry by Kim Almas   8/28/2013

We were able to see him briefly, and now he's off getting a follow-up mri. He was really hungry, and trying to get steak :-)

(The nurse agreed to toast.) :-)

Long Day
Journal entry by Kim Almas 8/28/13

It's been a long day. Before I say anything else, I wanted to say thank you: to our family and pastor who were able to be here with us and with the boys today; for all the encouraging texts, posts, emails, etc., from countless other family and friends; and for other ways friends have stood in the gap for us. We appreciate your love and support more than we can find words to say.

Now for the update. The surgery itself was considered to be a success. The resection was even better than the surgeon himself originally thought. Mark is alert and joking :) The boys were able to come in and see him, which was great.

However . . . there are some rough things to report . . .

* Because the surgeon needed to be more aggressive, Mark's already-weak right leg is even weaker now. We're looking at a significant amount of rehab there.

* His right arm and hand are also extremely weak, but that is caused by swelling in his brain, and should get much better in the next week or two. In fact, it's already a little bit better since a few hours ago. In the meantime, it's a good thing he's ambidextrous! :)

*And finally, while we won't know for sure until we get the pathology report back (probably Friday or Monday/Tuesday), the type and grade of the tumor (from what the surgeon can tell) is not as positive as we had hoped. It is very likely at least a Stage III.

Naturally, that was hard to hear.
But, we are staying positive and are gearing up to fight hard. We are grateful for the support of our family and friends, and most of all we are grateful that our hope is not in anyone or anything but the Lord. We have peace in the middle of this storm.

"When life is stormy,
it is so easy to doubt . . .
But I am learning that it is not
the lack of storms in our lives
that testifies of Jesus;
it's the Savior in the boat."

(unknown)

06

Game time

Once again Kim and I, my parents, and this time my oldest brother
and Kim's mom, found ourselves waking up extremely early in the
morning, driving to Boulder Community Hospital for brain surgery.
My father-in-law stayed at our house with Max and Zac. Cutting time
was scheduled to begin at 7am. It felt so surreal as we drove
into Boulder, as most people don't experience a single brain surgery,
and here I was in transit for a second, four years later.

We arrived at the hospital, filled out all the paperwork
to be admitted, said our "see you after surgery" to my family,
and Kim and I headed in to get prepped.

After getting fitted with my gown, they hooked up all the IVs
they needed for surgery and afterwards, shaved the squares of hair
needed on my head to attach the diodes needed to sync the last
MRI taken just before surgery to the Real Time MRI. This is the
last MRI that Dr. Nelson would see before cutting into my head,
used to position my head during surgery, and used following to
compare with the MRI taking following surgery, to double check
he cut out what he needed.

I left Kim in the prepping room and wheeled down to get my MRI.
The first room they took me to the MRI machine was broken and
being fixed. So they looked for another machine that was available.
This seemed to take forever, although it was just a few minutes.
I just wanted this over.

After the MRI, I was wheeled back to surgery prep and waited
with Kim for Dr. Nelson. As we waited, the nurses performed their
last minute prep, and we signed more forms. With other appointments
Dr. Nelson was prompt so this seemed out of the ordinary.

When he finally arrived, something was off. He always was serious, but today was more-so. I didn't let on to Kim my feelings, but I could tell Dr. Nelson was very concerned with what he saw on the MRI. One nurse realized we were Believers, and quietly sang an old Christian song.

What we didn't know was that in the few weeks between seeing Dr. Nelson's face larger than life on my iPhone and now, the tumor had grown exponentially.

After a little small talk, Dr. Nelson started to read off the last set of forms, basically relieving him and the hospital of any legal obligation if something went wrong, even death – then we signed them. I said my goodbye to Kim, gave her a kiss, and left her and my boys in God's hands.

There are so many medical people that play a role on a brain surgery team. I believe mine had 13. Of course you have the surgeon, his physician's assistant, nurses, anesthesiologist, along with many other -ologist's. I don't understand how they get so many people into such a small space to work.

During surgery the bed transforms so you're in a seated position. Mike (PA) was positioned near my feet, touching and requesting me to do different things then watch my reactions. I have no clue all he asked me to do or what we talked about. I'm sure it wasn't politics, I would have flat-lined. Before surgery I asked him if he would take a few pictures. Hey, who has pictures of their brain?

During surgery, they took a slice of tumor and placed it under the microscope. They could see the tumor cells replicating in real time. Dr. Nelson pretty much knew he was dealing with a Grade IV GBM, or Glioblastoma Multiforme.

After his part of the surgery was complete, Dr. Nelson met with Kim and my family in the waiting room. He let them know I was out of surgery and getting prepped to move to recovery. He prepped them for seeing me. He told them he was very confident it was at least Grade III but most likely it was Grade IV GBM (This was the first we'd ever heard that phrase. Kim knew those three little letters would forever change our lives.) He went on to tell them I would not be able to walk, let alone stand, again. He went on to say "he wouldn't have done any more or any less if it was his wife or child." He reminded them it was a quality of life issue.

I can't imagine what the end of his day looks like. He literally holds life in his hands ... and the personal fallout. That is stress.

A wise man once reminded me during a sermon, describing doctors, "doctors practice medicine." They don't get it right 100 percent of the time. We hold them in such high regard, almost God-like, but doing brain surgery... come on. I'm just glad my surgeon knows personally the One who gave him his gift, and not afraid to give Him the credit.

Remember how I asked my PA to take pictures? Check out the next couple of pages.

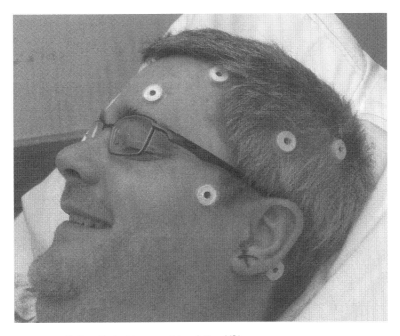

REAL-TIME MRI Diodes attached to sync with real-time MRI

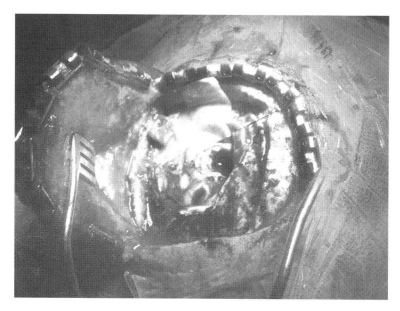

SURGERY 01 Clamping skin back

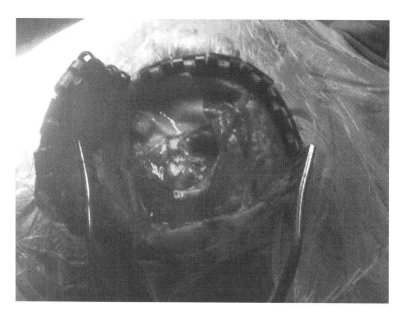

SURGERY 02

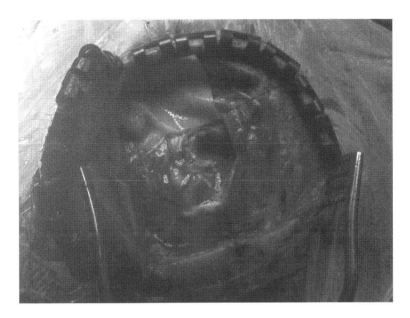

SURGERY 03

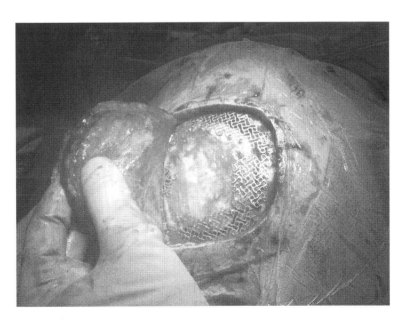

SURGERY 04 Closing

I like to scrapbook, but this is ridiculous.
Journal entry by Kim Almas 8/29/13

Mark has been very tired today, but otherwise
is doing well. He was able to move to a chair
for a while, and the pt/ot techs were pleased
with his strength and mobility, in spite of
the weakness on his right side. That was
encouraging!

He was also just moved a few minutes ago
out of icu! As wonderful as his care was there,
we're glad to be moving on so soon.

"Fun Fact" of the day: Did you know that
your surgeon (or in our case, his p.a.) will take
pictures of your surgery, during surgery,
and then email them to you?!?!

Um, yeah . . . I passed on that delightful viewing opportunity, but Mark was fascinated . . .

I'm sure he'll show you if you ask . . . (But trust me, those are not going into the scrapbook!)

~Kim :)

You're never quite prepared . . . and yet...
Journal entry by Kim Almas 8/31/13

Yesterday was a rough day. We got the pathology results back, and they were not what we were hoping for. It is definitely a Grade IV glioblastoma. While we knew that that was a strong possibility, I don't think anyone is ever quite prepared to hear those words.

And yet . . . as awful as that sounds, and as hard as it is to wrap our heads around, we are still who we are at the core. We still know our God loves us and is walking this with us. We still trust Him 100%, and even anticipate healing.
He still has the whole thing under control, and wasn't remotely surprised at the news we heard yesterday.

So, now what?

Mark is already in rehab to get him mobile, and to get his arm and hand working.
The people here are terrific. If you have to be in rehab, this is the place to be. He's doing amazingly well, and we are hopeful that he'll be home sooner than we originally anticipated (but we'll see).

(Side note: As I'm sitting in the little kitchen area typing this, I just saw him walk ~ with help ~ past the window!)

There are lots of decisions we need to make, some sooner than others. One of the most important things we're researching is our treatment options. There are about a half-dozen things we are seriously considering. Please pray that we have wisdom as we decide.

We've had some friends come visit, which really boosted his spirits! If you think you might like to swing by this week, let me know so I can work it around his therapy schedule. (But seriously, no pressure! Just wanted our friends to know it's an option.)

Finally, please pray for our boys. They are handling the news admirably right now, but it could get rocky. Please pray that they will only grow in their own faith in Christ through this.

Thank you, friends, for all your love, care, and support! I know I'm repeating myself constantly with that, but it really does mean so much to us.

"The Lord gives strength to His people; the Lord blesses His people with peace."

Psalm 29:11 (niv)

So how about some positive news for a change?
Journal entry by Kim Almas 9/3/2013

Mark's been doing great in rehab, and is continually amazing his therapists and doctors. His arm and hand are coming back slowly, but they are definitely coming back. We are so happy about that!

But the truly incredible thing is how well his leg is doing! Today he was actually walking down the hall with a walker, with only minimal support to his weak arm, and nothing helping his leg except for his normal brace. (If we're FB friends, I'm going to try to post a video, so watch for it!) And then he topped that off by walking down the hall completely on his own, only holding on to a rail on the wall!

When his surgeon came in this morning (even before all that) to check on him, he was completely stunned with what Mark had been doing in rehab, and with what he was observing just in the room! His eyebrows raised way up, and he grinned hugely, and said, "I am shocked. You should not be able to do this! I know what I took out, and you do not have the connections from your brain to your leg to make this happen!" And as he was walking out the door, he turned and said with another huge grin, "You just made my day!"

It's just a completely miraculous answer to prayer. There is no other explanation, and we are praising God. Thank you for keeping on praying!!

In other news, apparently since he has such a large entourage, they moved him to a much bigger ginormous corner room today, with huge windows and a gorgeous view of the mountains!

Life.Is.Good. :-)

07

Recovery

Kim is a rock. After hearing potentially devastating news,
she was able to come stand by my bedside with the best poker face,
with her amazing love and tenderness. I can't help but think what
must have been going on in her mind knowing that our life was
about to change, big-time. As much as I wanted to know the
outcome of the surgery, she was able to divert my attention away
from all the "what ifs." She didn't even let on the severity.

One by one, family and friends who kept Kim company through surgery came by to visit me. The expressions on their faces were as you would expect, seeing someone after a major surgery. Still under major drugs, I did not pick up on anything they were just told in the waiting room.

My brother Mike, who had flown from Sacramento, CA, to be with me, Kim, and the boys for surgery, was scheduled to fly back home the morning following surgery. When he said goodbye to me before leaving, he teared up as he reached the door, turned, and said, "I love you, Mark." I joked with him later this was the first time I knew it was bad. You see, in my family – four boys and one girl – little did we show emotion or say "I love you" to each other. We knew we did, and we knew we'd be there for each other, but saying those words, "I love you," was not a common thing we said to each other.

Still in a fog, I started to notice things not working like before. I realized that even though I was moving my right leg in my mind, nothing was physically happening. My right arm – moving in my mind, but only in my mind. Trying to close my hand, touch my fingers to my thumb, was just not happening. That was the first "Houston, we've got a problem" moment. After my first brain surgery I had weakness on my right side, but not to this extent.

It was very helpful to keep my mind off things as one by one, family and friends, who gave their time to support Kim in the waiting room, came by to see me, if only for a few minutes.

Later that night, just before closing my eyes, Dr Nelson came by to see how I was doing. After the normal chit-chat, and running me through his patient routines, he let Kim and me know there was a very good chance I developed a blood clot or aneurysm (something that can develop during brain surgery) and if I did, I would be dead by morning. Being under great meds, or experiencing true peace that only comes by knowing Jesus Christ, we didn't give it a second thought. We knew God was in control. Kim climbed up onto my bed, rested her head on my chest and squeezed my hand, as Dr Nelson left the room.

I did wake up the next morning! -- **Miracle #1**

When I woke up, I was very hungry. Still in recovery, the nurse told me to take it easy. After a small breakfast, I believe a piece of toast, I was encouraged to sit in the chair beside my bed. It took a few nurses quite a bit of strength and effort to transfer me from my bed to the chair. I was complete dead weight. It didn't take long for me in this position to lose my breakfast and for them to have to change my gown and transfer me back to bed. Nurses work so hard. They jump in to do nasty jobs, and get little thanks. Mike Rowe of "Dirty Jobs" has nothing on my nurses. In bed, realization was getting more apparent as to how much therapy I was going to need, still not knowing all that Kim knew.

The next day my parents brought Max (age 13) and Zac (age 11) to see me. I remember them carefully climbing on the bed and laying on me. It was special. I knew they were scared, and this was the fist time I would be able to let them know everything was going to be just fine.

All day and the next I was bounced from recovery room to recovery room as they searched for an open bed in the therapy wing. That entire time Kim remained so strong. So strong, I forgot how bad things could be. I had no sense that Kim, Kim's dad, brother,

and sister were already working on treatment options/plans, etc. –
they are wired that way. My family can build beautiful houses
and solid businesses, but this is thinking on a whole other level.
They were being proactive not knowing the exact result.

Kim and my dad were in my room when Dr. Nelson and his PA, Mike,
walked into the room. Of course we all were waiting the diagnosis,
so the focus quickly turned to them. After very little small talk,
he told me I had Grade IV GBM (Glioblastoma Multiforme).
Dr. Nelson said I had 12 to 16 months to live – as he teared up,
I told him I was going to prove him wrong. I remember Mike sitting
at the foot of my bed, just dropping his head .

After Dr Nelson and Mike left my room, there were some tears,
but I most remember feeling "now we know what we are dealing with,
let's get after it, hard." My dad left Kim and me alone. She crawled
onto my bed and we just laid there in the presence of God,
knowing He's in control. There is not a medical chart available that
will change God's plan.

The following song has been the heart song of mine, this entire
season:

Hope in Front of Me

I've been running through rain
That I thought would never end
Trying to make it on faith
In a struggle against the wind
I've seen the dark and the broken places
But I know in my soul
No matter how bad it gets
I'll be all right

There's hope in front of me
There's a light, I still see it
There's a hand still holding me
Even when I don't believe it
I might be down but I'm not dead
There's better days still up ahead
Even after all I've seen
There's hope in front of me

There's a place at the end of the storm
You finally find
Where the hurt and the tears and the pain
All fall behind

You open up your eyes and up ahead
There's a big sun shining
Right then and there you realize
You'll be all right

There's hope in front of me
There's a light, I still see it
There's a hand still holding me
Even when I don't believe it
I might be down but I'm not dead
There's better days still up ahead
Even after all I've seen
There's hope in front of me

There's a hope still burning
I can feel it rising through the night
And my world's still turning
I can feel your love here by my side
You're my hope
You're the light, I still see it
Your hands are holding me
Even when I don't believe it
I've got to believe
I still have hope, You are my hope

Strategy Time!
Journal entry by Kim Almas   9/22/13

We've had a good week at home! Mark feels
a little bit stronger and sees improvement in
his right side every day. He was even able to
get back to work some (he works out of the house),
which he loved! So we are thankful!

We've been researching treatments like mad.
Honestly, it's pretty overwhelming to have
to sort through it all . . . We're thankful for
family and friends who have been helping
us! We've prayed a lot for wisdom too, and
have felt your prayers.

At this point, we've decided that a combination
of strategies is our best approach.

First, we got him back on Essiac tea. You can Google it for more info, but we strongly feel that it's effective, for several reasons. (Not the least of which is, he had been taking it since the last surgery, up until about 6 or 8 months ago when we ran out. Up until this past July he had clear mri's. Things that make you go, "Hmmm...")

Next, we got him going on several Shaklee supplements which are targeted to help him get stronger and heal. If you're not familiar with Shaklee, I'd encourage you to check them out. I can't say enough good things about them!

In addition to all that, we are making baby steps each day toward eating healthier (more veggies, less sugar and dairy, etc.).

Then, we decided that the first actual "treatment" will be to have him do at least one round of chemotherapy (probably Temodar) and radiation. In many ways this was a difficult decision ("surely there must be a "natural" way that is just as effective!"), but overall it makes the most sense to us. About 80% of our research and counsel highly recommends it. And, because we are working with a limited time frame (humanly speaking), we just want to hit it hard and fast.

There are still some loose ends to either tie up or pursue for "what's next," but as it stands now, we'll meet with our oncologist on Tuesday (9/24/13) to get set up for the chemo/rad. We'll share more details when we get them, but we've been told that for about the next

6 weeks, he will take the chemo once a day (a pill), and have the radiation Monday through Friday.

We're praying that the Essiac and Shaklee will aid in his healing, and keep him feeling good while he's going through the chemo/rad.

Once we're through that, we'll decide what to do next. Clinical trials are a strong possibility. We've already talked with a doctor at University Hospital about getting him in on a trial of the Novo ttf-100a (It's an external device that looks kind of like a swim cap full of magnets. It's supposed to mess with the north/south poles of the cancer cells so they can't reproduce.) There are other options we're seriously looking into as well (a friend's doctor in Florida, the Bursynski clinic in Texas, other clinical trials with vaccines and viruses, and much more).

So please keep praying for healing and for wisdom! As stressful as this all is at times, we still joke that we could feed him a Fruit Loop diet and God could still easily use it to heal him. We do the best we can to research and plan and attempt, but ultimately we have full confidence and peace that we are well-cared-for in His hands.

Sorry this was a little long! I'll finish up with a nod to our friend Jaime, who shares updates on Facebook about her baby boy this way each week :)

Highlights of the week include: going to church (one of about three places he's allowed to go right now); letting the boys give him a "buzz" haircut (which I think they enjoyed just a little too much, hehe); and picking another theme song, "Good to Be Alive" by Jason Gray. Here's a YouTube link: www.youtube.com/watch?v=qdoquTXwonM

Enjoy!

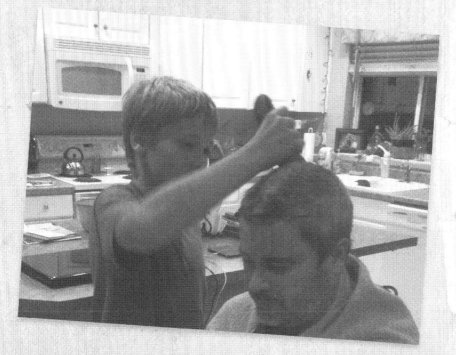

117

08

My wife

Kim is amazing. She is the perfect example of a Godly wife. There is no doubt God gave her to me. It's so easy for me to point to her and tell my boys that's who to look for in a wife. She is compassionate. She is kind and caring. She is selfless. She is my best friend.

When I was in grade school, I remember the parents of a friend of mine were going through a divorce. Watching what that did to him, I remember praying, "God let me know, without a doubt, the girl

I marry someday is the girl you have for me." I wanted to make sure that no matter how big our difference of opinion is, I would have no doubt she is the right person for me.

Kim will tell you we met shortly after her family moved to Sacramento. She says she remembers me being upset when my dad asked me to take her family out on our boat and teach them how to water-ski. We were at a church family camp and I wanted to go skiing with my friends, and I guess it showed. She said she thought I was a real jerk.

I think we met, the first time, after a basketball game we were at for the high school I just graduated from. Following the game, a group of us went over to Kim's house. On the way there, I was riding with a friend of mine. I found a Lifesaver on the floor of his car. Sensing a challenge and noticing the sunroof of the car Kim was in was open, I wondered if I could hang out the passenger window, driving the "speed limit," at night, and drop it through the sunroof of her car. It came off my fingers smoothly, lofted up into the air, looked to be on target . . . as I lost it in the night sky. Bummer! When I arrived at her house, was she upset. Not only did I get it though her car's sunroof, I placed it in the middle of her forehead. So basically I threw a rock at her, hitting her in the forehead doing about 40mph. She thought, "what a jerk." I guess you can pick whichever story you like, but either way, Kim ended up marrying a real jerk.

Being Christmas break, a few days later we went on our "first date." After dropping her off I remember leaving her house and thinking, I am going to marry her one day. When I asked for another date, before she went back to school, I was told no. During the Easter break I heard she was back in town so I asked her out, and she said yes. When I asked to take her out again before going back to school, she said no. Summer was coming and I got thinking here's my chance to get a second date. Can you believe once again, "yes" on first ask and crash and burn on follow through.

It had gotten back to Kim's mom that I said I was going to marry her one day. In college, Kim got engaged to another guy. I would see her mom and she'd ask, jokingly, "What's up? I thought you were going to marry my daughter?" It started out as a long engagement. As time went on, Kim's prayer turned to asking God if 'Mr. Right' was the right guy for her. Well … we both laugh now, but Kim and I were about to have both our prayers answered.

You see, Kim had an extensive stay in the hospital following being misdiagnosed with the flu, turning into a severe case of pneumonia then staph. While family stood beside her bed emotionally drained, expecting life-support to be hooked up any minute, 'Mr. Right' demonstrated he was not going to take care of her like she'd want. God answered Kim's prayer.

God also answered mine – you see, there is not a day I wake up without seeing the scars on her back, and not be reminded God gave her to me. The doctors had to scrape out the lining of her lungs to get a handle on the infection. Her heart stopped beating three times on the operating table. The scars that remain remind me daily that God saved her for me.

Kim is an incredible teacher. When we first married, she was a fourth grade teacher at a small Christian school in Fair Oaks, California. It was fun bumping into her students and/or parents and being told that Kim was their child's most favorite teacher – "Yep … that's my wife."

When we had our own children, we decided to homeschool. Kim wanted to now invest in our own children now. I'm so glad I didn't fight her on this. Our boys have turned into incredible young men, and I credit her.

We had the best field trips. Being self-employed I only needed
cell service and a laptop to work. Kim worked up her lessons plans,
then we'd plan trips to see the places they were studying. This made
for many adventures along with making learning fun. We had never
seen the colors of New England; we saw them. Visited Niagara Falls
(that's a lot of water), of course taking pictures all along the way.

I remember being on the replica of the Mayflower, on a conference
call talking to people around the globe, looking around and
thinking, "Here I'm on a cell phone; what must it have been like
a few hundred years ago?" Then turning my head, seeing my boys
climb around, talking with living history docents, watching Kim
in her element, loving every minute of it. Did I mention she is an
awesome teacher?

The boys had seen a commercial on TV that said the best lobsters
come from Maine. We had dinner in Maine. We learned there is
a big difference between warm-water and cold-water lobster,
and also that in Maine you have to dress up in a big red lobster
costume when delivering lobster to the table. Very fun time.

We learned how real syrup is tapped from trees, and that there
are three grades. We ate ice cream at the Ben & Jerry's factory

in Vermont, and down the street, my mom bought the boys each a Vermont Teddy Bear. In Boston we bought the boys "authentic" tricorn hats. Walking through the city they broke out singing "Yankee Doodle Dandy" at the top of their voices, all 4 verses (who knew there were 4 verses?). Smiles broke out as people watched them walk down the street. A very special memory for me.

Spending time at Disney World, Kim used it for homeschool. Epcot is a treasure trove for making learning fun. I love how Kim has conditioned all of us that learning never stops. We took a cruise

FIRST DAY OF SCHOOL Zac Preschool; Max First Grade

to visit Mayan ruins and swim with dolphins. These experiences have allowed Max and Zac to make friends all around the world, who they keep in touch with to this day.

My boys were homeschooled. They are very smart, socially adjusted, and both have black belts in Tae Kwon Do (I wouldn't talk down homeschool to them). In 2018 we watched our oldest, Max, graduate from high school (under the authority of a private school). In 2019 he studied Japanese in Japan, and is now attending Tokyo Christian University. We watched Zac begin college at 16 years old. We always say he can make friends with a rock, and he brings the fun. But he is also a very creative, solid, thoughtful young man who we are so proud of. Once I thought he would follow after me in graphic design but now I could see him designing web apps. He is currently attending Grand Canyon University, majoring in Computer Programming. I give Kim the credit.

I am so proud of Kim. Kim is my Rock Star. She spins so many plates. Wife, mother, teacher – now caregiver. When I promised Kim for better or for worse, how did I know how much better I would receive. Now that we entered into this new season of life, once again Kim finds herself having to step up.

Boys throwing rocks
into Lake Agnes.

Studying how power is
made at Niagara Falls

Having fun in an old
Colorado ghost town

I love watching Kim use every
opportunity to homeschool

Max and Zac loved the Ranger Program available at most National Parks

An amazing woman, educator, wife, and best friend. A favorite place of ours is visiting the Garden of the Gods just outside Colorado Springs

Cook's Farm Dairy

Dinosaur Ridge, CO. where we touched actual dinosaur footprints

Science is fun!

Biology class made fun

Not so sure about snakes

What kinda bug is this?

Walk like an Egyptian

Studying Native culture

Assignment: write a short story

Physical education class

2009

Meeting Kit Carson's great grandson

Extreme geology 103

Visiting Kim's grandparents in Canada

CHIPCHASE

WELCOME TO
MAINE
The way life should be

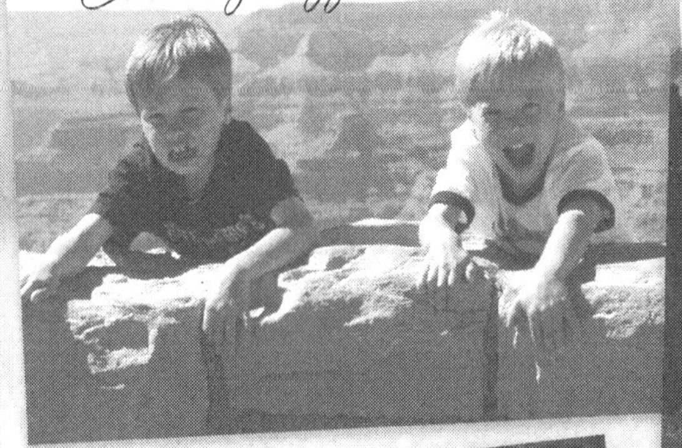

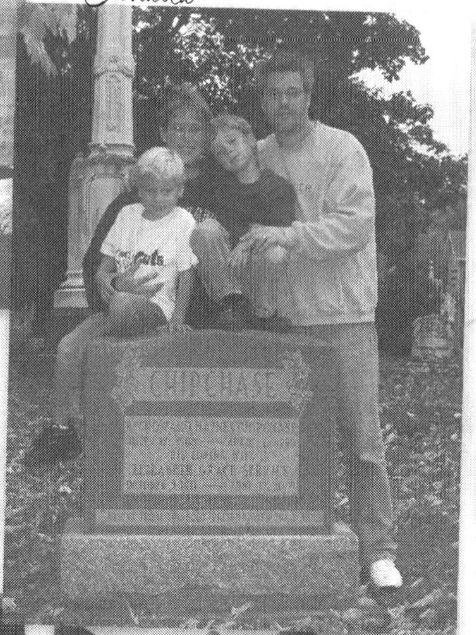

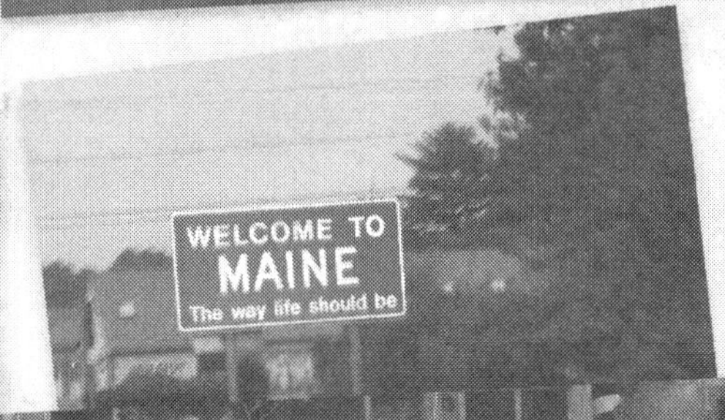

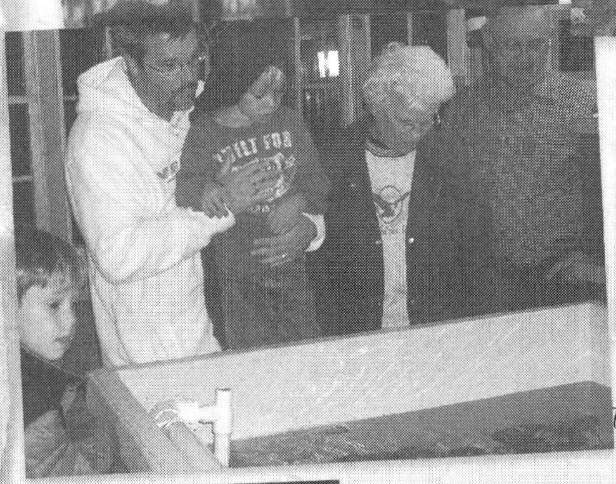

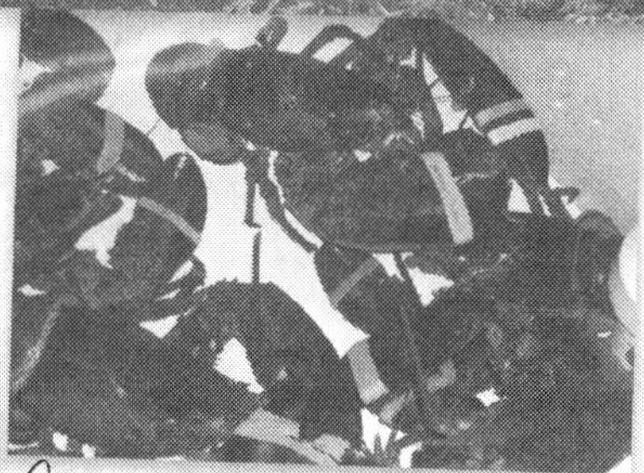

Max and Zac heard on TV the best lobster came from Maine. We had to see for ourselves.

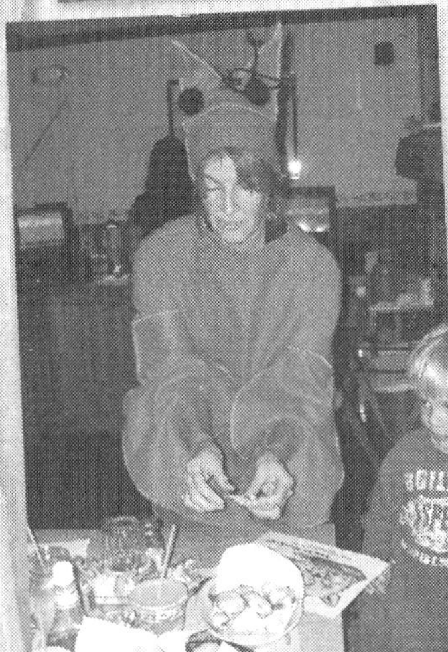

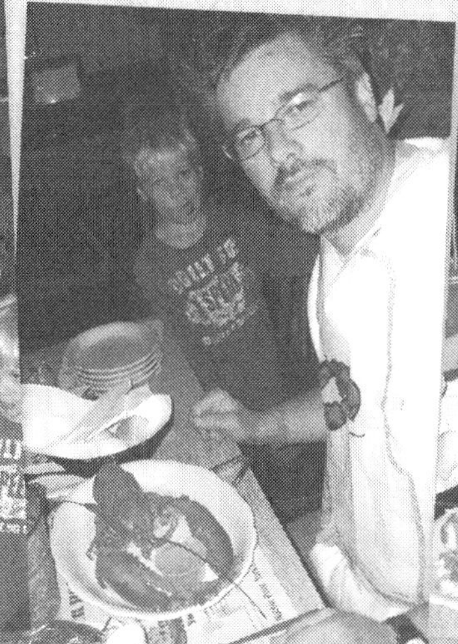

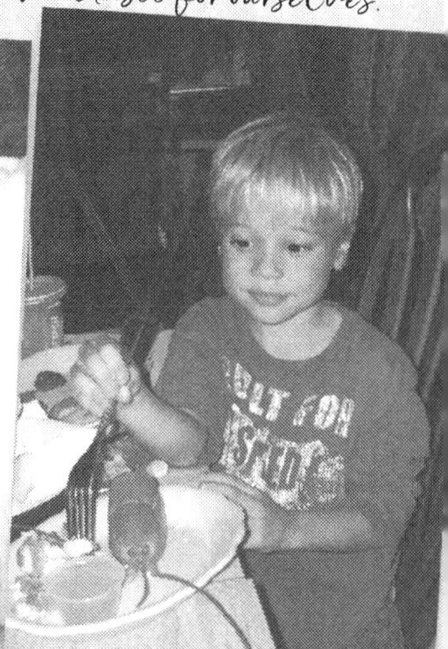

So cool seeing a replica of the Mayflower and being able to climb on and through giving Max and Zac a different view on what it was like on that transatlantic cruise

Imagining the trip aboard the Mayflower.

Actual Plymouth Rock

American Stonehenge

We love living history!

Watching Max engage with this Native American woman was incredible

These Native Americans took the time and had the patience with our boys to explain the conditions of the period

Down-time playing in a authentically made canoe

George Washington's pew

Old North Church, is the location from which the famous "One if by land, two if by sea" signal is said to have been sent.

Betsy Ross' house

Frame of Ben Franklin's house

WIND CAVE
NATIONAL PARK
VISITOR CENTER
AND
HEADQUARTERS

Jr Spelunkers Club

We had so much fun watching these bear
cubs playing on this dead tree.

The best field trips

When teachers go bad! (lol)

Personally, I thought they would be bigger (lol)

Can't get better hands on learning than this. Camping with your own private teacher

This extra time I've been given, I've seen both my boys grow into incredible young men and best of friends.

Where else can you get 535 people to agree on anything . . . yeah right . . .

One of the many beautiful paintings in the capitol — this one in the capitol dome.

George Washington's burial place

Sitting outside the most powerful house in the in the world

Mt. Vernon, the home of George Washington

WWII memorial.
Very big, beautiful
and well deserved.
I can't imagine what
you experienced, but
thank you for securing
our freedom.

The Jefferson Memorial
A favorite of mine to see at night. Iwo Jima

FDR memorial
A nod to Depression era food lines

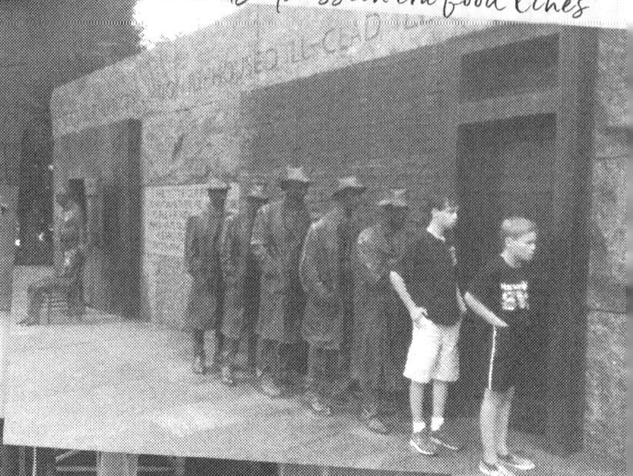

The SR-71, my favorite airplane.

sr-71
Blackbird
in front of
Space
Shuttle

In a relatively short amount
of time, seeing the progression
from the Wright's flyer
to the sr-71 is mind blowing

The Enola Gay reminds
us even though we have the
power to, we have the power
not to use it

1903 Wright Flyer

AIR FRANCE

United flight 93 memorial.
"Let's roll." Todd Beamer

Things are moving along here!
Journal entry by Kim Almas 10/2/2013

The pre-chemo/radiation appointments that
we thought would be this week actually
happened late last week, and we are on track
to start everything tomorrow ((October 3)!

I don't think I mentioned it here before,
but some of you may be aware that we've been
having a problem with our insurance
company, Humana, not wanting to cover the
chemo drug, Temodar. Their reasoning is that
since it's in a pill form, it's a prescription;
and since we don't have prescription coverage,
we pay for it out of pocket. Um, what?!
Everyone at the Rocky Mt. Cancer Center
(rmcc) is puzzled, since it's clearly a
treatment and not just a normal prescription.
You can't even get it at a normal pharmacy!

Anyway, today we verified that we have an 11th hour treatment solution! Kim's brother, Jim, turned us onto injectable Temodar. This form of Temodar Is covered by Humana. The crazy thing is it will cost them between 3 and 5 times as much money as the pill, but they will not cover the pill. Go figure.

Mark's oncologist continues to fight Humana on our behalf. He will start treatment tomorrow, regardless. Radiation is at 1:15, and the chemo infusion begins at 1:30 and will take 90 minutes. Radiation will be every weekday for the next six weeks, and the chemo will be every day (including weekends) during that same time. If our oncologist can get Humana to see the light, he will be seamlessly switched to the pill form of Temodar.

So this is a very big answer to prayer. Treatment will be covered by our insurance.

And, even though the chemo infusion is not as "easy" as taking a pill at home every day, it's still not terrible. There are comfy-looking recliners, wi-fi and coffee are available, and the view of the Rocky Mountains is pretty terrific (especially with the fall colors now!).

(But, please still pray he can switch soon! Thanks!)

I hope to update again tomorrow, to let everyone know how it went!

Kim, experiencing one
of her favorite rescue
stories of all time,
"The Hiding Place"

Family at
Glacier Bay,
AK

09

Therapy

Sunday night my treatment schedule was posted to my wall and outside on my door. The first day began the official evaluation to determine what type of therapy I would need. During each session I would be evaluated, and later therapists would gather to discuss my case to determine what treatment I needed.

Monday I woke up, had breakfast, then fell back asleep, all before my first Speech Therapy (SP) session. The therapist came to my room

REHAB SCHEDULE

NAME: **Mark**
DAY: **Saturday**

ROOM #: **406**
DATE: **8/31/13**

MORNING		AFTERNOON	
7:00		12 – 1	
7:30		1:00	
8:00		1:30	
8:30		2:00	PT
9:00		2:30	
9:30	OT Eval 1	3:00	PT
10:00		3:30	
10:30		4:00	
11:00	OT	4:30	
11:30	PT Eval	5 – 6	

SAMPLE SCHEDULE Posted inside and outside room

at 10am and woke me up – you sleep a lot with brain injuries.
For this session we did therapy in my room. We spent time talking
and playing various games. She was specifically looking for issues
with my speech, and my thought processes. I spent 30 minutes
talking and playing games with her – I didn't even have to leave
my bed. Games like Traffic, Sudoku, Mazes ... all geared to make
me think in different ways. When she left, she told me she would
recommend to the team I not be required to attend Speech Therapy.
This would open up time for treatment better suited for me.
She left, I fell asleep.

Around 11am, I was awakened by my Physical Therapist (PT).
We chatted for a few minutes, then she requested additional help
to transfer me to a wheelchair. After strapping me in, we headed
down the hall to the therapy room.

We got to the door and I was
expecting to be wheeled over
to the table mat as this was
how we began following my
Grade II Surgery – not this time.
They rolled me to a machine
that looked like a treadmill
with a bunch of straps hanging
from the ceiling. As they hooked
me into the harness system
and lifted me up and over
onto the treadmill, a Seinfeld
episode came to mind – the
one where Jerry is at the
airport being wanded by TSA,
feeling totally embarrassed
says, "People, I deplore you."

The harness system provided me zero gravity. Now remember, nobody had told me I wasn't supposed to stand or walk, "ever again." Left arm and leg not a problem. Right arm dangled, and right leg dragged for a second before my therapist physically picked up my foot and became my interim brain moving my foot forward. We worked out for about 15 minutes, then wheeled back to my room where I collapsed from exhaustion.

After my nap, lunch was there waiting for me. I was not able to eat it all before my next therapist showed up in my room to introduce herself.

Occupational Therapy (OT) was my last session for the first day. OT focuses on everything above the waist. We did this session in my room. Most of our time was spent picking up and moving various sized blocks around my bed table – picking up was more like tapping and sliding.

The therapy team reconvened later that day to discuss my case. It was agreed I did not need Speech Therapy, so they doubled me up on both Occupation and Physical Therapy. I was one happy camper.

It became an inside joke for when I did something stupid, I would usually follow it with "don't send me to speech therapy."

They knew about my previous experience, and we were making light of it. Sometimes they would joke back and say, "Wow! You may need some speech therapy."

A few days into therapy, Dr Nelson came by to check on me. He was running me through his paces, asking me to respond to various tasks. He asked me to move my big toe. When I tried, there was a little movement in my right leg. He jumped back and said, "Do that again." Even though it was just a little, he said, "You can't do that! I cut out the part of your brain that controls that function." Because nobody had told me, I remember thinking, what's the big deal? As he walked out of my room he murmured, "God is so good." -- **Miracle #2**

During the next few days my "fan club" grew. Kim kept people who wanted to visit me informed of my schedule as not to wear me out. Mid-week my social worker, Lisa, came by to see how I was doing. She was amazed how many people we had in my room. She stepped one foot inside the door, and said, "Oh, this will not do," turned and walked back down the hall. A little concerned we had more than our room would allow, she came back a few minutes later, letting me know they were moving me to a larger room. I was in the hallway

working out with my therapist when I saw my bed go by ... then my
night stand ... then the last of my personal items. Following therapy
I was taken to my new room. It was huge. It was created by the
generosity of "a previous family" for families transitioning to their
new normal. Looking around I was simply thinking, "wow" – and then
fell asleep from exhaustion.

Waking up, I realized I was in a corner room with two sides full of
glass windows looking toward the mountains. The room was five
to six times the size of a regular room. The view was incredible.
Later that evening Lisa came by to ask if "my room was suitable?"
with a big grin. I jokingly replied, "So this is the room you give to
patients that are about to die" – remember she had been with me
through two brain surgeries, she understood my sick humor.
She let me know what the room was designed for and that with the
number of people coming in to see me in my previous room,
she joked we would run into fire code problems. She made sure
therapy would not need this room for the foreseeable future,
then had staff move all my stuff down the hall into it.

One by one guests came by to visit me in my new digs. They were
amazed with the size and view. As they gazed outside though the
windows at the beauty, inside I was saying, "Hey, I'm over here!"

PARTY TIME Still restricted to bed, we celebrated my mom's birthday.

Kim kept tight tabs on my therapy schedule and it was always good seeing people, especially after a good rest.

I have missed many of my mom's birthdays (being with her in person) living in Colorado and her living in California. One night we celebrated my mom with a surprise birthday party from my spacious hospital room. We opened gifts, had cake and ice cream. Just a normal birthday, but at a hospital, in a hospital room. I'm sure this one was more noisy. Even though I was confined to my bed, it was great to put aside the heaviness of life if just for an evening.

All my nurses were incredible. One in particular was a night nurse from the Philippines. Her name was Maria. She told me she preferred the night shift – she said she had more liberty at night to care for her patients. She always entered my room with a smile, making me feel like everything would be OK. She would bring me dark chocolate candy bars. One night she asked what my favorite food for dinner was. As I stumbled, with my words, Kim responded, Rib-eye Steak. Maria said she wanted to bring Kim and me dinner the following Wednesday night. We had no idea the gift we were about to receive. She set the conference room table up with a

DATE NIGHT Rib-eye steak, corn on the cob, broccoli, rice, shrimp cocktail – Thanks Maria

white tablecloth and place setting for Kim and me. Her brother grilled two huge Rib-eye steaks, the vegetables and corn-on-the-cob were grown in their garden, mashed potatoes, shrimp cocktail, sparkling juice … the works. In the middle of dinner Kim and I remembered this was our weekly date night. Maria, not aware, was being used by God to bless us. Best date night ever.

The following days were filled with therapy and plenty of relaxation. Each day I was getting stronger. I was able to spend more time doing therapy on my own from my bed. I still was experiencing severe weakness on my right side, now known to me as hemispheric paralysis.

I now had graduated to walking with a walker – well kinda. My right hand was secured by Velcro, a therapist to each side of me and a wheelchair followed directly behind me, in case I ran into problems.

Each day we made further progress down the hall, many times with Kim and my mom at the end cheering me on. OT occurred in and outside of my room, pending her goals for me for the day. Some days we would slide blocks around, up and over other blocks, all targeting the parts of my brain to reengage.

Days were full of therapy, rest, and visits. Nights were filled with broken sleep. Every few hours, either a nurse would come in and give me medicine or just to check on me. Some nights I would fall back to sleep quickly. Others, not so much. Unfortunately this gave me time to think of the "what ifs." I have confidence in my destination for when I die. I know God will take care of Kim, Max and Zac, and that God prepared all of us for this time because the Bible says so. I know without doubt we'll be together again when we all get to heaven. I guess it was during these "pity parties" I focused on things I would miss being a part of – graduations, weddings, grandchildren…

It was during one such pity party a very young nurse entered my room to check on me and found me crying. Not knowing what to do, she quickly finished her job and left my room. It turned out to be a very good cry. God met me there and reassured me of His promises, and I was not doing this journey alone. A few hours later she was back in my room. I apologized to her for the moment she found me in earlier. She apologized for not knowing what to do or say and hurrying out of my room. She then asked if she could pray with me. Wow! So quickly God assured me, I was not on this journey alone, from a nurse I never saw before, and I would never see again.

Over the next week, therapy targeted getting me home – quality
of life. For PT this meant going outside on walks to introduce me
to various surfaces. Each day I would put on a safety harness,
grab my walker and head outside. I now know exactly how my
dog Moose feels before going outside – Walk! Sidewalks look
so innocent, but when you least expect, they jump up and grab you
– not cool. Stairs were another thing that kicked my butt.
No more hurrying up … or down. Ascending, I had to concentrate
on not catching my toe on the upward step lip. Going down,
I had to concentrate, going one step at a time – left foot down,
right foot down, repeat, left foot down, right foot down.

OT was mostly playing with blocks and other games to continue
engaging my brain. We did do some exercises in the kitchen to see
how I would do – not a good idea for a hemispheric paraplegic
to be around sharp objects – lol. We practiced picking up paper
and other everyday items. The funnest sessions had to be
playing Wii – until she insisted I play with my weak arm. Wii bowling
turns out to be great therapy, just saying.

The therapist at BCH worked hard on me so I would have the best quality of life leaving the hospital.

Some sessions very hard. Some tiring. All very worth it.

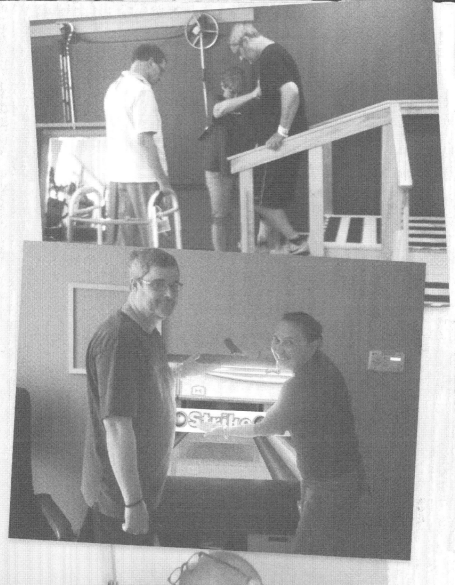

Erik Petrik —
Work associate,
friend

10

Coming home

When I got the word I was signed off to go home, I was so excited. The therapists were awesome but I wanted to be back with my family in a bad way. I knew I had outpatient therapy ahead, but I wanted to sleep in my own bed. The morning started with breakfast, followed by getting the staples pulled from my head. You don't feel them while they're in but when they come out – ahhh, relief.

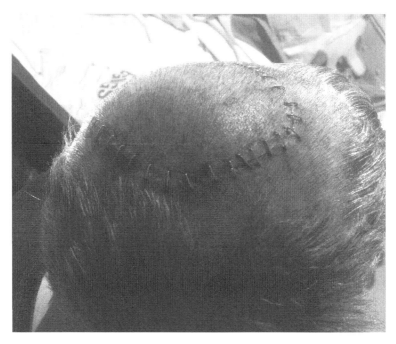

STAPLE REMOVAL 27 staples – over half less than used in my first surgery.

Kim was there around noon to pick me up. After all the paperwork was filled out, outpatient treatment scheduled, I was discharged and we headed for "freedom." Seeing my car pulled up under the receiving area was a beautiful sight. Little did I know there was one more therapy session – getting in my car, an SUV. It took a half a dozen determined tries, but I made it. We left the hospital for home. Pulling out of the parking lot, it seemed everything was new, even though nothing had changed. Boulder is a beautiful city nestled up to the Rocky Mountains. It seemed more clean and beautiful today.

The first thing I had to do on the way home was to stop and pick up medication. Waiting for Kim in the McDonald's inside Walmart, I looked down at my right wrist and noticed all the wrist bands attached while in the hospital – "Allergy." "Fall Risk." "Faith." While I waited, I reflected on what I just went through. Few people go through one brain surgery and now I'd been through two. Sitting there looking at these bracelets, once again I'm reminded of God's love and faithfulness.

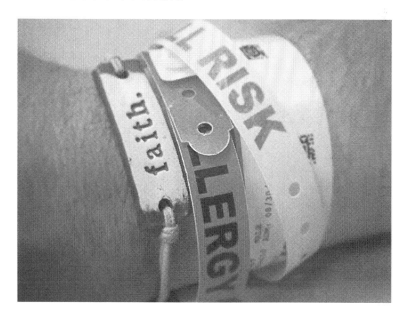

Walking back to the car I noticed the weather had changed from sunny to cloudy. It looked like one of our afternoon storms was about to start. Getting home I was greeted by a "Welcome Home" banner, my family, and Moose, our 2 year old puggle.

Getting things started, Kim had scheduled an oncology appointment the very next morning. It was very early when we left. None of us bothered turning on the TV to see the weather or traffic report. Totally unaware we were in the middle of a 100 year storm, Kim's dad, Kim and I headed for University of Colorado, Anschutz Medical Campus, Aurora, CO.

Due to all the flooding, we were about an hour late to my appointment. Dr. Damek was amazed we braved the elements. She help us formulate a treatment plan. Chemotherapy and radiation would be performed at Boulder Community Hospital, because it was closer to where we lived, and back to her for maintenance, MRI's and evaluations. Barely finishing this introductory visit, evacuation alarms went off at the hospital.

Driving home didn't take as long as driving there. Still, a trek expected to take 30 minutes took a couple hours, pushing water much of the way. Only when we got home and started watching the news did we see how bad the storm was. If I hadn't gotten discharged from the hospital when I did, who knows when I would've. I was told there was a 10' wall of water that came through the canyon near the hospital hours after I left. With the room I was given,

I would have had the best view, although it would have certainly delayed my release. Parts of the main cafeteria were under water, and doctors, nurses, and other staff were unable to drive in due to roads being flooded and bridges being washed out.

The next day my scheduler, Kim, started setting up my home therapy. I was under house arrest. Other than treatment or therapy, I was not to leave the house. They figured if I could go outside I did not need outpatient care. A couple weeks in, I was going stir crazy. My brother and sister-in-law came for a visit. At that time of year, the Aspen are changing colors. How much trouble could I get into going on a drive, right? The first stop, as I was getting back into my van on the passenger side, I reached out to close the door and fell out of the van. It happened so fast. I had gotten in, reached out for the door with my weak-side arm, and before I knew it I couldn't breathe. It totally knocked the wind out of me. The last time this happened I was in grade school. A stranger who was just ahead of my brother saw me fall. He rushed over and along with my brother picked me up and help me back into my van. I was so embarrassed. Still with difficulty breathing, I was beginning to learn my new normal. How to accept help. Also, how to work up an excuse for my case worker so we didn't lose out on home therapy care.

One day I went outside on a walk with my therapist. With walker
and security straps, we carefully walked down the few steps leading
outside my house. I had been in therapy for a few weeks, getting
stronger every day. I made it about six houses down the street
before my energy was zapped. When I turned around, there stood
a neighbor so excited to see that I was walking, but didn't want to
interrupt my therapy. We talked briefly, then my therapist
and I headed back to my house where I collapsed in my recliner.

As I rested, I couldn't help but think how special the neighborhood
we lived was. One neighbor, Deb, organized meals for us, for months.
Another brought me a blue, very soft, oversized blanket. She told me
it was for the nights I couldn't make it up the stairs and would
need to sleep in my chair. Others drove Max and Zac to Tae Kwon Do,
mowed our lawn, shoveled our snow, sent gift cards …

Our family was incredible too. Beautiful railing was built by my
brother, Dave, so I could safely get up/down my stairs. Other family
who came to see us did odd jobs around the house, cleaned,
made special organic/healthy food (or just food I craved), helped
with errands or took the boys places.

Other friends sent encouraging cards, notes, books, music, etc. The friends I work with in Austin, TX, sent me a care package containing a bunch of fun swag along with a team picture standing behind a banner saying "We're Praying"... on and on I could go about the love I felt looking around me. So much support. So many people taking this journey with me and my family.

SAFETY RAILING My brother Dave used his skills to install this beautiful railing system.

Looking into the treatment that I would need, Kim and I quickly realized that we no longer fell under our insurance policy. Our policy covered the surgery but not pharmacy. Radiation was covered, just not the chemotherapy. Huh?

We were facing an out-of-pocket expense of over $3k per month. That's a big nut to crack. This was in the middle of the heathcare changes to "O'crapcare" and nobody seemed to have a clear idea about the new rules and regulations. Even though I was not in an "O" program, it changed everything.

The day before I started treatment, I had to get fitted for my radiation mask. This is not made to protect me from the radiation but to hold my head in position while the procedure takes place. Just before leaving for the hospital, an out-of-state friend unexpectedly drop by. I told him what we had to do, he jumped in the car and we were off. He was in town for just a few hours, so this was my first "mobile visitor."

After the radiation mask was made, I returned to the "love and concern" of Kim and our friend Steve, only to have them look at me and start laughing, hysterically. What I didn't know was in making the mask, it left a grid pattern all over my face. This pattern remained for quite some time. So a simple glance would start another round of laughter. Only when I got home did I see what they were laughing about – I did look bizarre.

NEED OF A LAUGH Being fitted for the radiation mask

It was literally in the eleventh hour when my brother-in-law,
Jim (who works in medical research), called and asked if the cancer
center would administer my Temodar via IV and if it was the same
as the pill. We called and they confirmed they could, and that there
was no difference between the Temodar pill and IV, except now
it would be covered by insurance. So … let me get this straight.
Insurance won't pay a $3,000 per series for a pill because in their
system it's categorized as pharmacy, but will pay over $35,000
per series for me to be hooked up for a couple hours to an IV,
because in their system is categorized as treatment? Same drug.

I started treatment the very next day. I walked into the room;
was helped up onto the table; head positioned; mask put over face
and radiation began. Radiation took about 20 minutes.

Following, I went upstairs to start my first round of chemotherapy.
This took longer, as I had to get an IV hooked up and mix the
chemotherapy (chemo) drug. Once the chemo was flowing,
it took about an hour. I would block out a couple hours each day
for treatment. This went on for eight weeks. Five days a week for
radiation, 7 days a week for chemotherapy.

I finished my first round of chemo/radiation before Christmas.
Believing most likely this would be my last one, we decided
to spend it in California where my entire family would be.
We spent a solid 3 weeks with friends and family.

Christmas was special. My entire family was together. The first time
in I'm not sure how long. We did some singing. Kim led in a
devotional – we knew I would not make it – emotions were high.
We ended by handing out to each family a plaque, saying, "In Christ
alone my hope is found. He is my light. My strength. My song."

Later that night, my sister-in-law asked me, "How can you do this,
go through this, have such peace?" This put me back on my heels.

We both were raised in similar families, with similar values. As much as she was asking me how I could have such peace, I was thinking, how can you not? God promises to provide. I guess these are the times we find out how strong our faith is.

Personally, I don't see how anyone goes through something like this without a personal relationship with Jesus Christ. If things turn south for me, I know where I will spend eternity.

Returning home, I started and completed 12 months of chemotherapy. At my last appointment, I was made aware I was a "guinea pig." The nurses and doctors had been carefully watching me. You see, I was the first patient to take Temodar via IV under their care. They were amazed at the lack of side effects I was experiencing. I was asked if I would be willing to continue an additional 6 months.

One of the side effects I experienced was being very fatigued starting mid-week. Also, smells of some foods would make me not want to eat. Because I wanted to lose weight, I saw it as a good thing, I called it my chemo diet.

Home Sweet Home!
Journal entry by Kim Almas 9/10/13

We brought Mark home today! Still lots of therapy and treatment ahead, but for now, we're loving just a little slice of "normal." :)

Many thanks again for all your prayers and support!

Kim

Home Sweet Home
Arriving home to my family
and two year old,
very "excited" puggle.

Austin team bling:
(LEFT TO RIGHT) Rick Kern,
Jeff Koay, Maris Naylor,
Beth St. Paul, Sam Klatt,
Cora Rodenbusch,
Leah Green, Austen Menges,
Ginny Jensby, Troy Springfield,
Brooks Birdsall, Joey Moore,
Jason Demetri, Erik Petrik.

An interesting and productive day
Journal entry by Kim Almas 10/11/13

Yesterday ((Oct. 10) was unexpectedly
productive and informative! We drove back
down to University Hospital for a follow-up
appointment requested by the doctor in charge
of the clinical trial we looked into a few weeks
ago (Dr. Denise Damek). Long story short,
we ended up signing up for the trial, which
is for a device called the Novo ttf-100a.
Since a picture (or better yet, a video) is worth
a thousand of "my" words, here's a Ted Talk
that explains exactly what it is: http://www.
ted.com/talks/bill_doyle_treating_cancer_
with_electric_fields.html

Mark has a 2-out-of-3 chance to be chosen to use the device (along with another round of chemo administered concurrently), and a 1-in-3 chance that he would be in the control group, using just the chemo. Since he was already going to do another round of chemo anyway (barring a miracle!), we figured he might as well sign up for the trial in hopes that he will be chosen. Also, if we decide at any point that he shouldn't be in the program, he is free to leave it (for example, if we come across another treatment that appears more promising).

And then it got interesting . . . Turns out Dr. Damek might have a way to get Humana to pay for the Temodar pills!

She recently had a patient in the same situation (although that was the only other time she had heard of this). This patient's wife, a lawyer, said, "I don't think so!" and, after much research, found an obscure Colorado law that says that insurance companies can't do that (at least in particular circumstances . . .). Armed with that information, Dr. Damek wrote a letter to the insurance company, and the next thing they knew, their drug was approved!

So, Dr. Damek is going to be writing that same letter to Humana on our behalf! Please pray that this is the answer to our prayer.

We also got the go-ahead to add Melatonin to our regimen. There are some very compelling articles out there, from both sides of the "medical opinion aisle," on its effectiveness in fighting cancer, as well as alleviating some of the negative effects of chemo (without hindering the work of the chemo). If nothing else, it should help him sleep better, which in turn should give him more energy throughout the day.

Speaking of negative effects of chemo, Dr. Damek also let us know that by now Mark would be feeling all of whatever he is going to feel from it! That was great news, because we were expecting him to get progressively more crummy-feeling, and overall he's really doing well right now! He has only had minor, fleeting nausea (which he hasn't even had to take meds for), and some tiredness/fatigue during the day. The radiation will still probably make him more tired, the longer he's doing it, but that's manageable!

And finally, some last minute news we just received today: both of his therapists signed him off of the home care, so he is now out from under "house arrest," which we are very happy about :) Not that he's ready to do a whole lot, but he's looking forward to at least feeling free :)

THERE'S **HOPE**
IN FRONT OF ME

Maris Naylor is an amazing designer
and young woman that I'm proud to call friend.
Even though my work with her has ended,
we continue to stay in touch.

11

Making memories

I made my first business trip back to Austin, early December 2013 to attend a Christmas party for a company I was a contractor with, along with Kim. Before the party started, Erik asked Kim and me to join him in his office. He reminded me of our time on his boat as a team just before surgery. He asked me if I remembered what I said if it came back as Grade IV. Then he asked, "What's your plan?" After I realized he was not talking about my contract but in my family making memories, I was speechless. Kim and I were so focused on treatment, we had not planned anything. He encouraged us to go dream. The next morning, Erik and his wife Kelly, took Kim and me to the airport. As we said our goodbyes, I leaned over to Erik and said "cruise" and "history." He just smiled.

As we were planning for our trip, in late January Erik called and apologized for not connecting with us on Christmas, to let us know the CEO wanted to pickup the entire cost of our dream trip and to connect with the company's travel agency – mind blown.

We started with a 12-day Trans-Atlantic Disney Cruise from Florida to Barcelona, Spain, which was followed by a little trek through western Europe. From Barcelona, we spent a week in Paris, a week in Normandy, a short time in Holland, and then six days in London. Highlights included special access to the Mona Lisa, dinner at the Eiffel Tower, sharing the 70th anniversary of D-Day with men who stormed the beaches, and getting pictures with my boys saying "thank you" and shaking their hands. Other highlights were accessing and standing in the closet where Jews were saved from the Nazis in the Corrie ten Boom House, and seeing Stonehenge. It was truly an amazing time for us, and we were able to make some irreplaceable memories that we'll carry forever.

Thank you Erik for encouraging us to take the time to do this and your help to make this happen financially.

This whetted my appetite to travel and make more memories. We went to several niece/nephew weddings in California, visited friends in southern California – great memories.

We had never been to Hawaii, so off we went. Honolulu is a beautiful place. Of course we saw the normal tourist spots, but a high school friend of mine, David Young, who was in the military hooked us up with a behind the scenes personal tour of Pearl Harbor. I was not able to, due to the weakness on my right side, but Kim, Max and Zac toured an Ageas Class warship – Zac loved sitting in the captain's chair. While my family toured the warships, our host took me to the other side of Pearl where a fleet of subs were docked – awesome. Again, not able to go inside safely, I was able to

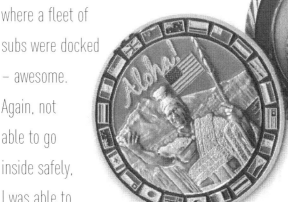

see a fleet of subs following war games. Not able to take any pictures, all I can say is these things are huge.

Another guide David set us up with took us to an area few see. We saw where the bullets hit when the Japanese zeros flew by knocking out some of our sea planes. As we drove around Pearl

NATIONAL CEMETERY OF THE PACIFIC Thank you for your service Great, Great Uncle Owen – meet you in heaven.

WHEN IN HAWAII ... you have to go to a Luau

she pointed out where various military leaders lived the day we were attacked and other fun facts. She showed us the flag that flew over Pearl Harbor that day, bullet holes and all.

At the National Cemetery of the Pacific, I was able to find the name of my great-great uncle, who served on the USS Franklin as a fireman. While under a torpedo attack, he was blown over the side, his body never found.

I'm sure you can tell by now, I love history and seeing it come alive in my two boys is a very special memory for me.

CELEBRATION Too much fun celebrating Mom and Dad's 50th anniversary on an Alaskan cruise.

Still under the influence to "go make memories," we shared
my in-laws' 50th wedding anniversary on an Alaskan Cruise. Sure,
some things I was not able to do because of safety, but I could sit
in my wheelchair and watch Kim, my boys, and the rest of Kim's
family walk around the glaciers. Seeing them laugh, their smiles
large on their faces, are memories I hold dear. Good times.

Max, from a young age, has had a "beyond his years" love for
all-things-Japan. In 2017, as a family we tagged along with his online
Japanese class on their urban backpacking trip through Tokyo
(thank you, Sensei Charlotte!). So much out of our comfort zone,

JAPAN Selected 1 out of 5 students from around the globe to attend Tokyo Christian University.

we saw him come into his own. Still not sure what the future holds, but if I am still here, I believe I will be visiting Max, living in Japan. In the Spring of 2019, he took Japanese language classes in Tokyo. So glad I was able to see him in his environment – also great memories. Update: we found out that Max was selected one of five students from around the globe to attend Tokyo Christian University, in Tokyo, Japan, beginning fall of 2020.

I am so glad I was encouraged to make memories. These are the lasting images Kim, Max and Zac will hold to after I am gone. Sure, I hope to be here for many more years so I plan to make many more.

We started our dream trip by taking a 12 day, transatlantic Disney cruise from Port Canaveral Florida to Barcelona Spain.

Perfect Trust

Charles R. Swindoll

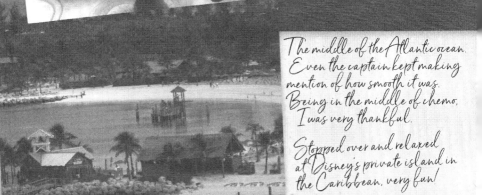

The middle of the Atlantic ocean. Even the captain kept making mention of how smooth it was. Being in the middle of chemo, I was very thankful.

Stopped over and relaxed at Disney's private island in the Caribbean, very fun!

One of our favorite excursions was
Mamas and Tapas in Malaga

Built in medieval times, staying overnight at one of the many Mont St. Michel hotels alongside the cobblestone road leading to the top, to the abbey, is very cool. You enter by crossing a heavy wooden draw bridge built in the 900's, walking down a narrow cobble street, shops both sides, narrowing to a single wide walkway up to the abbey. The boys had a blast exploring with Kim while I took a nap. I can't tell you how many very cool places I slept. Recovering from brain cancer, you need sleep and a lot of it. I didn't want Kim or the boys to miss anything so we agreed if I needed, they would carry on without me. Staying here was such a cool experience and memory.

This is just one example of God one-upping us. Experiencing the 70th anniversary of D-Day w/ the greatest generation, awesome!

Omaha beach, and memorial.

Cliffs of Pointe du Hoc.
Out of the 225 Rangers
to start the ascent,
only 90 made it to
the top, able to fight
— amazing.

Thank you, just isn't enough!

R.I.P.
JUNE 1944
TO THOSE BRAVE MEN AND WOMEN
OF THE ALLIED FORCES AND RESISTANCE WHO
TOOK PART IN THE LIBERATION OF
NORMANDY.

Dave & Suzanne Marty,
thank you for buying us dinner
in the Eiffel Tower

Better than front row seats to
the Mona Lisa.

Coming across this street entertainment was the icing on the cake.

I love watching Kim in her element — home school never stops.

Zac is our class clown.

Sitting in this spot, it's hard not to think about all the history that took place here — people being beheaded; sentenced to time in the tower.

Both Max and Zac loved goofing around with this English style telephone booth and in the Sherlock Holmes museum, cabs and other forms of transportation.

This has to be one of the coolest museums ever I've seen in my travels. It's like the war was over, everybody stood up, turned the lights off and left the room not to be disturbed until about 20 years ago.

So cool!

Big Ben, larger than life!

Stonehenge, built by aliens (lol), an ancient society still an impressive site to see.

I love paying attention to the various graphic approaches from around the globe.

COUNT YOUR BLESSINGS

Max and Zac wanted to see actual windmills. Very cool to see them for the first time and through their eyes.

Many Jews were saved by people stepping up and putting their lives ahead of their own. Above, in a closet, as many as 10 people at a time. Below, in a secret room, 6 families.

Mmmmmm. Ice Cream Cone

Standing on the USS Arizona memorial this flag blowing strong in the wind, I was filled with mixed emotion. I live free today because of the brave men entombed below

Damage left by the Japanese zeros at Pearl Harbor _ ground/wall

My wife threw me a surprise
50th birthday party while on a business
trip in California. I loved seeing
friends I had not seen for years.
A birthday I did not expect to see.

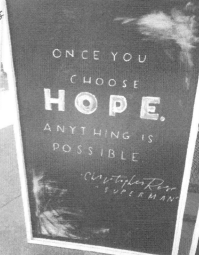

So true!

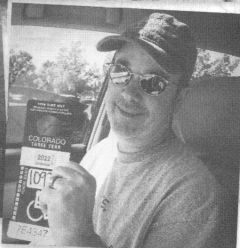

Teaching Max and Zac to drive

Outliving my crip card extension.

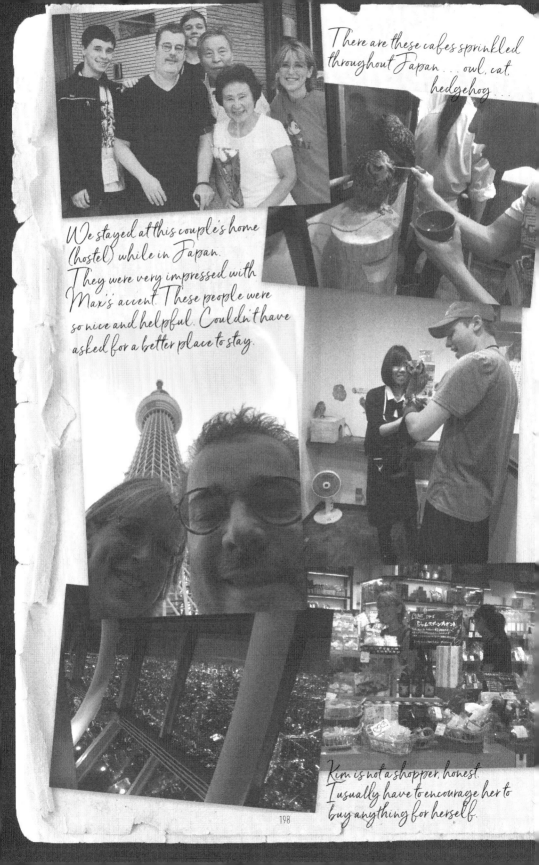

There are these cafes sprinkled throughout Japan . . . owl, cat, hedgehog . . .

We stayed at this couple's home (hostel) while in Japan. They were very impressed with Max's accent. These people were so nice and helpful. Couldn't have asked for a better place to stay.

Kim is not a shopper, honest. I usually have to encourage her to buy anything for herself.

So out of my comfort zone we spent time at an Onsen. It actually was pretty fun. Great food, relaxing in hot water, fish nibbling at your toes... relaxing.

Couldn't understand a word but the music, the costumes were stunning.

This couple owned the store that was around the corner from our hostel - very nice people.

"In Christ alone my hope is found,
He is my light, my strength, my song;
This Cornerstone, this solid Ground,
Firm through the fiercest drought and storm.

What heights of love, what depths of peace,
When fears are stilled,
When strivings cease my Comforter,
My all in all,
Here in the love of Christ I stand."

And the rain fell and the floods came

and the winds blew and beat on that house

but it did not fall because it had been

founded on the Rock. Matthew 7:25 (ESV)

12

Healthcare heroes

Surgeons and doctors tend to get all the credit. I'm thankful for them but also to the entire surgical staff and beyond. The receptionist checking me in. Her professionalism and calmness began this experience on the right footing.

The pre-op nurses. With the delays caused by the real-time MRI, they stayed focused and on point helping us get all the forms completed. They were relaxed and fun under the circumstances.

Post-op nurses – letting you know where you're at coming out dazed from anesthesia.

"Cleanup in Recovery Room #3." Recovery nurses have a tough job. No sooner than they get one mess cleaned up and I'd make another. Not like there's ever a good mess but you are special people to clean up after or change the clothing of someone not related to you.

There are nurses upon nurses that make sure you're comfortable. Nurses that make sure you are pooping and peeing regularly. Tracking how much is going in and how much is coming out. Taking it to the lab, returning with the results.

Nurses that administered medication (now in your best Homer Simpson voice, "Mmmm drugs"). They make sure you're getting the correct medications, in the correct amounts, at the correct times.

I did have one night nurse (looked to be 90 – a skeleton with skin) that worked a couple of weekends who would come in around midnight to check my vitals and give me my meds. She would wake me up opening the door, use a flashlight to bump around my room, give me my meds, then just as I would start to drift off to sleep (thinking she had left the room), she would shine her flashlight directly into my eyes. Startled, my body lifted off the mattress.

She would ask, "Anything wrong?" My thoughts, "You think?"
I look back at those nights now and laugh. A perfect storm.
The visual sight of this older nurse – the quietness of the room –
the sudden bright light shined directly in my eyes … I'm sure this
nurse meant well and has a big heart but this was a bad surprise.

The therapists were incredible. The Speech Therapist, Occupational
Therapist and Physical Therapist, were true professionals. The teams
worked together and focused on my quality of life. These are the
unsung heroes of my experience.

The techs making my radiation mask – administering the radiation.
Tech/nurses mixing then hanging my Temodar medication.

So many people … all with unique gift-sets.

I thank you for the extra time you given me to be a husband,
to be a dad – the memories.

The news we've all been waiting for...
Journal entry by Kim Almas 12/10/13

The mri looked good!! Praise God!!

We got a message from Dr. Damek's office (neuro oncologist with the clinical trial), and then later had it confirmed by Dr. Nelson (surgeon). Dr. Nelson said that he can't say definitively that there was no progression, but considering what he saw on the interim mri back in November, he was pleased. In fact, he kept saying, "This makes me really happy!" and, "This is as good as we could have hoped for!" Coming from him, that says a lot.

Next up: please pray that Mark gets the NovoCure cap, and isn't placed in the control group. We should find that out on Thursday.

And, please still pray that our insurance would cover the chemo pill! (He will be on a 5-days-on and 23-days-off chemo cycle for the next several months.)

Thanks again for all your encouragement and prayer!

Best Receptionist
Deb greeted us each visit, with her warm smile and welcoming tone, making us feel everything was going to be all right.

13

On another note

One day, as he was accessing my port, a male nurse at the cancer center asked me, "I've seen you here now for about a year; I've hung your chemo, but never asked you what you're being treated for." You should have seen his face when I said GBM. He followed, "How do you remain so positive?" I responded, "The way I see it you have two choices: be bitter, angry, mad, feel cheated; or believe God has a plan for me and nothing I can do, will change that plan.

I choose the latter." He sat there stunned, processing what I just told him. But that's just how I see it. What does being angry do?

When I check out support groups, I see people that are hurting. People who are bitter. People mad and angry, some thinking there's no hope. I see a lot of people just trying to get by, make it through. The word "beast" is used over and over again to describe GBM. I understand why and in some ways, I agree. But, I have confidence in what's in-store for me.

I had breakfast with my son the morning before he left for Japan for 3 months to study and be immersed in the Japanese culture. I am very proud of him. He has such a love for the Japanese people. With a future not certain for either of us, I could see the concern in his eyes if I would be alive when he returned. Using this same

Father/Son gifts given to Max and Zac just before leaving for college.

confidence I assured him that I wasn't planning on going anywhere.
But, if I was not here, I would look forward to seeing him again
in heaven and meeting all the people Max was able to provide
true peace to.

So, what comes next. I feel the need to be very straight forward
and blunt. There is a very real heaven and a very real hell.
For those who choose to believe there is a Savior, Jesus Christ,
will spend eternity with me. Those who make the choice not to
believe will spend an unimaginable, painful eternity. The Bible calls it
an eternal lake of fire.

I believe the Creator of the universe is waiting with open arms,
to receive me following my death. Why? The Bible tells me so.

I believe what the Bible says, that:

- God sent his son, Jesus, to earth in the form of
  a human baby.

- Jesus Christ died on the cross, for all my wrong doings (sin).

- Jesus Christ arose from the grave three days later.

- Jesus Christ ascended to heaven and now awaits me.

- I believe it is by faith and not anything I have done
  that gives me this promise.

I have this faith. I have found true peace. You can too.

By praying this simple prayer, I believe you also will be saved
and will spend eternity with me in heaven:

Jesus, I believe with all my heart, you are the Son of God.
I repent of my sins.

I know it is nothing I have done but you dying on the cross for me,
that I can receive your promise of eternal life with you.

I believe you conquered death.

I believe you were seen, by actual people, ascending into heaven
to take your place by your Father, and now wait for me with
outstretched arms.

I ask you now to come into my life.
Become the Lord of my life.

I believe if you believe or prayed this short prayer, you are saved.

[16]For God so loved the world that he gave his one and only Son,
that whoever believes in him shall not perish but have eternal life.
[17]For God did not send his Son into the world to condemn the world,
but to save the world through him. John 3:16-17 New International Version (NIV)

Now on the other hand, if you've read this far and think I'm crazy, I would encourage you to pray that God would bring clarity in your search for truth.

My hope is everyone reading this book finds true peace in Christ.

One year ago today...
Journal entry by Kim Almas 8/28/2014

One year ago today was, without a doubt, the worst day of our lives. I started to write a post about it, but realized that I really don't want to talk about all that . . . at least not the bad part . . .

I'd much rather think about the good things this past year brought :-)

Believe it or not, there are so many things to be thankful for, and I'd so much rather spend time thinking about that :-)

Because, as Ann Voskamp says, "There is always, always, always something to be thankful for" :-)

Like . . .

. . . the miracle of Mark walking, when the surgeon said it would be impossible

. . . the fact that he is still slowly getting feeling and control back in his right hand and fingers, which is also not supposed to be happening

. . . that he is still able to work

. . . that he was able to take Zac on his "12 year old trip"

. . . that the part of his brain affected by the tumor was not in an area that injured any vital body functions, nor his memory or personality

. . . the amazing and humbling love, support, and care from our family and our friends (near and far, old and new, neighbors and church, work and homeschool, and more . .

. . . the phenomenal trip we were given, and therefore priceless memories

And of course . . .
. . . the miracle of clear, unchanged, stable mri's up to this point

But most of all . . .
. . . realizing that when the going gets tough and the rubber hits the road, all the stuff we've learned and practiced our whole lives (spiritually) is legit, the real deal, and totally *works."

Wow. Pretty cool ... :-)

And a huge honor to be able to, in a sense, "prove" God's faithfulness ...

As a side note (but another thing I'm super happy and thankful about), I got the email today confirming that my Colorado teacher's license renewal was approved! This was a huge headache for me, and being able to move past that is a big relief. And that it came today, of all days? Another "wow" :-)

"In everything give thanks, for this is God's will for you in Christ Jesus."

1 Thessalonians 5:18 (nasb)

14

One of many opinions

Since I've survived over 7 years past surgery, I'm told I am a long term survivor. Even more amazing is that I've had no recurrences to deal with so far. So the question follows, "What are you doing for treatment (besides a darn good neurosurgeon)?" Essiac and prayer.

Essiac is an herbal tea I was introduced to in the late '80s. I worked on a book cover project, *Calling of an Angel* by Dr. Gary Glum, about a cure for all forms of cancer. I was skeptical, as I did not

think much of homeopathic remedies, until a story very close
to the studio I worked at unfolded in real-time. The account rep
from the book printer's manufacturer's nephew had leukemia,
and just had been given two weeks to live. I remember her barging
into our studio crying one day while we were in a design meeting
with the doctor. Gary started "hemming and hawing," I was thinking
"What a quack." What I didn't know was Gary was thinking how to
get the tea to her nephew without the doctors knowing about it.
Gary believed releasing the book in Canada would give cover for the
information getting out. He felt if the book was released in the
USA first, ingredients would become unavailable or illegal due to the
amount of money being made in cancer. I was told he went home,
made the tea, bought her round trip tickets to Alaska with specific
instructions how to give the tea to her nephew. I lost track of the
story about a year later, but the young boy was still alive.

My uncle was diagnosed with Grade IV Colon Cancer in 1981.
He was told to go home and get his things in order. He started
taking Essiac. That was over 30 years ago. He's still alive
and a great encouragement to me. Needless to say, I have a
whole new perspective about alternative medicines. Essiac is also
mentioned in many long-term survivor stories.

These days, Essiac comes in a pill form, dry mixed herbs, or a pre-made tea. I use the pills when traveling and the tea when home. You can buy Essiac in many health food stores or on-line. Three pills in the morning; three pills in the evening.

For the tea, it's 2 ounces in the morning and again in the evening. Kim purchases the ingredients online then brews the tea on a bi-weekly basis.

How to Brew a Small Batch of Essiac Tea

We use both Starwest Botanicals Organic Essiac Tea and Blue Moon Herbs: Essiac Tea Herbs (includes the stronger sheep sorrel root). Both are available on Amazon.

1. Bring 2 cups distilled water to a boil in a stainless steel or glass pan (not aluminum).

2. Stir in 1 rounded Tablespoon of Essiac herbs.

3. Lower heat, cover, and simmer for 10 minutes.

4. Remove from heat, and stir to get any herbs off the sides of the pan.

5. Cover and set aside for 10-12 hours (on the stove top or counter top).

6. Bring just to a boil.

7. Strain through a fine mesh strainer into your container. Store in the refrigerator. A little bit of "sediment" is normal; you just don't want big chunks of herbs.

8. To prepare, combine 1oz. Essiac Tea with 1oz. Distilled water. (Gently shake your container to mix in anything that has settled before pouring.) Microwave it for about 20 seconds to make it more like "tea" (or heat as desired).

Capsules:

Also good for traveling (or to have on hand if we run out of tea): Essiac Vegetable Capsules, available on Amazon (green packaging with picture of Rene Caisse, made in Canada).

Books (available on Amazon):

Essiac: A Native Herbal Cancer Remedy by Cynthia Olsen

Calling of an Angel by Gary L. Glum

Also working with a nutritionist has been super helpful for me.
I had a problem with sub-clinical nausea, loss of appetite,
and food aversion. It has been fascinating to learn how certain
chemo drugs kill certain taste buds; how my food aversion was
actually a type of nausea; and how to avoid or add certain things to
food to be able to eat more. Figuring this out has helped so much.
We used Nutritional Solutions (nutritional-solutions.net).
Generous friends arranged to pay for the supplements we purchased
through them.

132 Doses, Mint Chip Ice Cream, and a little Clarification

Journal entry by Kim Almas 5/8/2015

If we are Facebook friends, you probably saw that Mark had his last dose of the chemo drug Temodar today.

After 132 doses (!), over a period of 18 months, we were ready to celebrate and be *done* with it!

Big thanks to my mom and dad for coordinating the mint chip ice cream and balloons for our mini surprise party for Mark :) We were really happy to have Mark's brother and his wife (Mike & Mary), a couple of good friends (Rabs and Bob), and of course our boys there to celebrate too :)

I wanted to clarify a little bit about being "done" with chemo. Even though Temodar is the "gold standard" of treatment (along with radiation) for Glioblastoma Multiformee (gbm), there is still a deplorable lack of research that has been done with it. Typically, a patient takes it for at least 6 months, and often up to 12 months. That time span has been studied most, and seems to have the best results. However, there are cases where patients have taken it 18 to 24 months, but that is less common. There also seems to be a point where the Temodar stops being effective, particularly if the person has taken it for *too* long. Apparently it's a balancing act.

When Mark did so well with it for 12 months, the "tumor board" (a group of oncologists, radiation doctors, surgeons, etc.) concurred that 6 more months would be good to try. Basically, they said that it "might help, and couldn't hurt". They were also pretty much using him as a guinea pig though, since none of them knew whether or not it really would be helpful.

Another thing that was out of the ordinary was that he had to take the Temodar intravenously vs. taking pills (because of the insurance company). We found out today that this was a first for Rocky Mt. Cancer Center! They have been watching him closely, and have been very happy with how he has done with it (length of time tolerating it and lack of excessive nausea or other side effects, primarily). They are already starting to mention it as an option to other patients in our same situation! (A big shout-out to my brother, Jim, for researching this option for us!!)

In hindsight, based on all the good mri's, I would say that 132 doses of Temodar could very well have been something that God has used to keep the gbm away. It was pretty tough on Mark, but he pushed through, with amazing courage and determination and great faith.

He is my hero.

Could there be more Temodar or other drugs in his future? It's possible. We just pray it won't be necessary.

Today, we just celebrate being done with
18 months of this treatment!

You might say this is a "wait and see" stage
we are entering now.

But I think I prefer what a new friend
(and fellow gbm patient) recently told us:
Now we go live our new life, to the fullest!

Please pray that the Lord continues to keep
Mark on a path of healing, and that his
energy and appetite return.

Thank you for all the love and
encouragement, and mostly for the prayer!

~Kim

{Psalm 20:7}

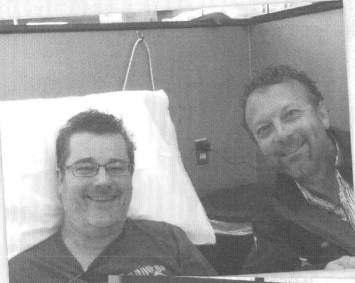

David Hughey,
"Rabs" –
Work associate, friend

Family (left to right)
In laws Jim and Anne Steel,
brother and sister-in-law
Mike and Mary, and Me,
Zac, Max, Kim Almas

Bob Bush –
Work associate, friend

15

Finishing day of doctors: Epilogue

We finish breakfast and make our way down the long corridor to the elevators at University of Colorado, Anschutz Medical Campus. Getting off on the second floor, we round the corner and check in at the front desk at the cancer center. More small talk with Kim, making fun of what we see on "The View," we make up our own script, to what they are actually talking about. Shortly, my name is called.

Mr. Almas? Meeting the nurse at the counter, I'm asked what year I was born, then walk through two large doors where I am weighed, then Kim and I are escorted to a small room where my vitals are taken. We're left in silence. It seems like forever, but I'm sure it's only minutes when Dr. Damek enters the room. We get caught up with her life since my last visit, then she asks if I have noticed any changes. After bringing her up to speed about the deterioration in balance, and the few falls I've taken, she starts checking my eye-tracking, she checks my reflexes, checks strength in my arms and legs, then watches me walk. Then, she draws our attention to the latest scans. She quietly scrolls through the scans before saying a word. Then the words we'd been waiting to hear, "No Change."

4 years ago today . . .
Journal entry by Mark Almas 8/28/2017

4 years ago today . . .

. . . I drove to Boulder Community Hospital for brain surgery.

. . . I arrived at the hospital and was prepped for surgery

. . . I was read the disclaimer of all that could go wrong during surgery by my surgeon (even death).

. . . I was rolled into surgery.

. . . I left Kim and my boys in God's hands.

4 years ago today . . .

. . . I made it through my second brain surgery.

. . . In the waiting room, Kim and my family were told most likely I had Grade 4 gbm.

. . . In the waiting room, Kim and my family were told most likely I would not be able to walk or probably even stand again.

. . . Not knowing the full truth, I watched my brother Mike tear up as he left my bedside, heading out to catch his flight the next morning.

. . . Kim and I were told in recovery, by my surgeon, that I may have a blood clot or aneurysm (something that can develop during brain surgery). If I did, I would be dead by morning.

4 years ago, plus 2 days, My surgeon told me I had 12 to 16 months to live.

4 years ago, plus 2 days, I told my surgeon I would prove him wrong.

4 years ago my family started a whole new season in life.

I am so glad God doesn't follow doctors' charts. Not only am I still alive, I am able to stand and walk (with help of a cane).

With the encouragement of a client, we have made many memories. We have literally traveled halfway around the world. Being a homeschool family, this has been the best field trip ever. God has one-up'd us all along the way.

I've also been able to be part of a project that's close to my heart, saving the unborn. Check out What If We've Been Wrong? hosea4you.org.

I've seen my boys learn to drive, get a job, succeed in school, and find their passions. Our prayer for them has been for all of this to draw them closer to the Lord, not push them away. And we are grateful that their faith is strong.

Kim and I were able to celebrate not just our 25th, but our 26th anniversary as well! And, a couple weeks ago I turned 50 -- a birthdate we didn't know if we would get to celebrate. Hopefully there will be many more birthdays and anniversaries to come.

I know some following my journey don't have a relationship with Christ. For me that is more painful to think about than the thought of not seeing my boys, graduate high school and college, meet their wives and my grandchildren. My hope, my prayer, is that all of you reading this will find the same peace I have experienced in life.

I knew God was awesome, but it wasn't
until cancer did I experience His amazing
"awesomenessness."

This may sound like a crazy term,
but I want to spend eternity with you all.

In His grip,
Mark

Max's Story

July 2013, was the month when my smile left. One day early in the month, my parents called Zac and me downstairs. They had a look on their faces that gave me a thought of what they were going to tell us, but I didn't want it to be true. My dad finally spoke, "The cancer came back." My heart dropped and I started to tear up. Shaking and in rage I made out, "Why…why us?!" My parents told us that it would be OK, but I was more than angry. I went back upstairs and started screaming at God, "WHY…WHY US AGAIN?!"

A week after we told our neighbors about my dad, the whole neighborhood came together and made meals for my family every week for a month. They also gave Zac and me gift cards to a game store to buy toys to get our minds off of the surgery and offered to give us rides to martial arts every week. They were so generous and I will never forget their kindness. My grandparents came back, took care of us and stayed at our house. More family came too to help out with house chores and to see dad. My uncles Mike and Dave built handrails for my dad for when he would come home, my cousins Justin and Vanessa took us for hikes in the mountains.

VISITING DAD First time visiting my Dad since his surgery

HE WAS SO PROUD Dad did live to see me get my Black Belt

We got to see him sooner than before because Zac and I were much older and we weren't sick. When we saw him, he was exhausted but he turned to the nurse and he bragged that Zac and I were Pre-Blackbelts in Tae Kwon Do, and he was proud of us.

I was happy he was alive, but I knew that my life would never be the same. A few days later we returned and celebrated dad getting through his surgery. It had been an emotional week and I was very drained and not spiritually sound. We were all happy that dad was alive, but I started hurting from the inside out.

I started getting angrier and angrier and sadder and sadder. I didn't want anyone to know how I felt so I put on a mask and started to kill off my emotions because I believed that emotions were causing my pain (I still was happy like on special occasions or traveling, but most days I was angry and sad).

Since I wasn't reading my Bible and I stopped praying (I still was a Christian and believed in God, but I did not act like one), I started hanging out with the wrong crowd, started to cuss my head off, and I had a giant hole in my heart that I thought I could fill with a thing that I thought felt good at first, but then became a nightmare (I'm not going to tell you what that addiction was in writing, but if you don't know what it was and would like to know, I will tell you). That thing made me feel sick, I felt like a piece of garbage, and most of all, it made me feel alone.

My dad was a Creative Art Director. One of his contracts was PGI, based out of Atlanta, with an office in Austin, TX. After his second surgery he was invited to their annual Christmas party. While there, he and my mom were encouraged by the CCO, Erik Petrik, to go make plans to make memories. Later, mid-February my dad received a call from Erik apologizing for not calling on Christmas but Boland Jones, the CEO of PGI, wanted to pick up the tab and to get in touch with the in-house travel office. Was I happy? Yes, absolutely, but I still was putting on my mask too, and was letting my addiction consume me.

In May of 2014, my family set off to Florida and met the ship at Cape Canaveral. It was a Disney cruise since we took one a couple years earlier to Mexico and absolutely loved it. I stayed in the teen lounge most of my days with my table mate, Josh, my British friend Damien, Greek friend Georgie, my two other American friends, Mackie and Griffin, and the rest of the teen lounge. Directly at noon, we would all look down from our window (since the teen lounge was in a fake smoke stack above the adult pool) and wait for the funniest sight to behold: when the clock struck twelve, the ship's horn would blast the "When You Wish Upon A Star" jingle and it would scare the crap out of the adults silently sunbathing in their European speedos (they totally deserved it for wearing that…yeesh).

Our first stop was at Disney's private island, Castaway Cay, and it was a water park on steroids and an entire island for us to explore and relax. After we left the island's port, we were on the high seas for about a week. Our next stop before hitting mainland Europe was the Island of Madeira, Portugal. It was a small island but had a big city along with farmland and really cool looking apartments.

After we left Madeira, our ship set sail again and went through the small strait between Spain and northern Africa! It was late at night and a few of my friends and I got to see Africa from the deck as we were walking back to our cabins. A day later, our ship stopped in Malaga, Spain, where we took a bus and went to the Andalusian mountains. Our tour bus stopped at an olive oil mill and we got to try olive oil on fresh bread! After we were done, we drove a little further and had lunch with locals who prepared us a true Mediterranean dish of beans and vegetables which tasted amazing. After a day in Malaga, our ship finally docked in Barcelona. We spent just one day in Barcelona, but took a double decker bus and toured to make the most of our time.

From Spain we flew to France, landing in Paris about two hours later. I was eager to see the famous city of Paris. We settled at our hotel and then hit the streets. Before we came to France, Zac and I saw an advertisement for the Pokemon Center Paris which was only going to be there for a limited time. One day, my mom, Zac, and I were taking a walk around and saw a sign for it just down the street!

That same week, my family went to the Louvre Museum, which was absolutely amazing! It was partially underground and in an old castle.

We got to see many famous paintings like the Mona Lisa which we got to see up close because my dad was in a wheelchair. We also were treated to dinner in the Eiffel Tower by some of our friends from Arizona!

A few days later, we packed our bags, and took a train to Normandy. It was the 70th anniversary of D-Day, and we got to see where the Allies invaded. I met many men who stormed those beaches and was able to shake their hands and tell them "thank you." I met one veteran who absolutely made my day. He was eating ice-cream

WWII HEROES I received this pin from a war hero who actually stormed these beaches 70 years ago. It was an honor to receive his salute and shake his hand.

by the beach and we made eye contact. I smiled and waved, and he gave me a salute with his ice-cream in hand. What happened next stunned me (and currently right now is making me tear up as a write this). He walked over to me and my family and started talking to me. He then reached into his pocket and pulled out a pin and said, "This is a special pin that I have only a few of to give to very special young men. This is the last one and I'd like you to have it." I was stunned. Special? Me? I couldn't be! I'm a failure! But it made me so happy when he said that he wanted me to have it.

After we stayed in Normandy and saw the different beaches and grave sites, we took a cab and went to the castle Mont Saint Michel, where we would stay the night. This monastery was built in the 900's but now remains an Abbey along with a small town below!

It was cool seeing the different old pathways and houses. Our hotel was built into the wall and had humongous omelets (which they are known for). Sadly, when we first got there, I again got bullheaded and got into a fight with my dad, and then got into another fight with my brother on the wall, and in public. I was so embarrassed. We patched things up, but I was still angry. I was letting my hurt control me again. I wish I had never let my anger control me.

After Mont Saint Michel, we took a train back to Paris and then flew to Holland. This would have to be one of my favorite countries. We visited Anne Frank's House and Corrie ten Boom Hiding Place, both were very inspiring. My mom had us listen to The Hiding Place audio-book before seeing the building where the Ten Booms hid Jews from the Nazis in a small, narrow, secret room behind a bookshelf. My brother and I got to climb inside and experience how small the space the Jews shared while in there – up to 16 people.

Next stop on our itinerary was England. I am a big fan of Sherlock Holmes and watched a lot of Dr. Who so I was super excited. We took the train from the airport into London, and got lunch in the train station.

After lunch we took a bus over to what was supposed to be our hotel, but when we got there, the room had no air conditioning, ground level, so we would have to sleep the window open, and people walking just outside could easily reach in – my dad said we would not be staying here, grabbed my hand to go look for a safer place to stay.

A few blocks away we found the Hilton Hotel that was connected to Paddington Station. We went back to get mom and Zac and left quickly. As my dad took a rest, we searched around the hotel and found the entrance to Paddington Station which had a bunch of restaurants and a Starbucks. My favorite restaurant was the revolving sushi bar that was right in the middle of everything.

The next day, we went to see Big Ben and rode the London Eye which gave us a gorgeous view of the city. The view from the London Eye was breathtaking! We could see the entire city from the top so I took a selfie at the very top. Later, we saw the Crown Jewels which were absolutely beautiful, and it was the first time I had ever seen legit treasure. Our tour guide was hilarious. Beside telling stories of historical events that happened inside the walls, good and bad, he told us stories about people asking him, "Are these the real crown jewels?"

Over the next couple days, we got to see Buckingham Palace, where we saw the changing of the guard, saw London Bridge from a river ferry, and went to see Stonehenge.

Sadly, our Europe trip came to an end, and we flew back to the United States. Seeing Britain was a great finale to our Europe trip.

And, now back to the real world. A few times, most times before the second surgery, and a couple times during the scare, I would get (what I call) a golden feeling, when I did pick up my

Bible and read. But I didn't continue regularly and went back to my old ways of being a very serious, angry, sad kid – I wore a mask.

My anger grew like a virus and got worse and worse to where I would scream and one time punched a wall. Part of the anger was because of my addiction, the rest was coming from my life as a son of a cancer fighter. Some nights I got very angry at God and screamed at him, "You don't really love me!" Or "I guess I'll stop worshiping you!" With my mask, my anger, my sadness, my dad, my addiction, my depression, and my terrible relationship with my brother, I became suicidal.

For a very long time, I had an obsession with politics. My mom was on Facebook one day and saw that the HSLDA (the Homeschool Legal Defense Association) hosted a leadership camp called Generation Joshua. She saw that one camp was down in Colorado Springs, so she asked if I wanted to attend. I signed up to be an ambassador for Japan because it looked a little easier than the Senate or Congress (plus it's serving Japan). So a couple months after we got back from our Europe trip, I packed my bags and left for the Springs. Although, even as we were on the road to the camp, my mask was fastened tight and I intended to keep it on.

After we arrived at camp and got checked in, my mom asked one of the staff who my counselor was. They said it was a guy named Chaz, who was setting up the worship tent. We walked down the path and found him. He was a buff, blonde, dude with a great sense of humor (he would eventually become one of my closest friends). I put my stuff in my cabin (Black Bear) and hugged my parents goodbye.

Every night we would have a chapel at the worship tent after dinner. My first few days, I sat in the very back and listened to the singing but didn't sing. The worship leaders were Daniel Heffington (Daniel

CAMP Not only is Generation Joshua a great leadership camp, it is located high in the mountains outside of Colorado Springs, CO – beautiful!

has two singles out now), Jill, and Mamie. During the first few worship nights, I tuned out and read the book of Revelation instead of listening to the speaker (I found out in 2017, from one of my mentors, Jeremiah, that he and a few leaders saw me in the back and were praying for me because they saw me hurting.) The night of the first chapel is where I met the rest of my cabin. Going off of memory, my cabin mates were David and Daniel (brothers), Caleb, Austin, Jordan, Tyler, Carter, of course Chaz, and a few other guys.

We did our introductions and then got to our wing chapel (which is a small talk about what happened in the big chapel and a few other things). Our wing chapels would go on for hours either talking about Batman, history, war, etc. which I loved to listen in on because of how some conversations became very interesting debates (mostly concerning Batman).

Our first summit meeting was where I met my new big sister, Jenae, who was the Ambassador for Argentina; the Ambassador of Taiwan, Elise, who was actually an immigrant from Taiwan who spoke Mandarin and French; the ambassador of North Korea, Johnathan, and the Ambassador from India, Marissa. A few of my cabin mates were also ambassadors, like Jordan was the Ambassador for South Korea and Austin who was the Ambassador for the United States.

Our mission for the summit was to retrieve a U.S. sub that crashed in North Korean waters without causing an international incident (if we started a war, we would fail the simulation). A few times I zoned out (which was kinda embarrassing), but I was forgiven and everyone wanted everyone to have a good time solving the world's problems.

In the middle of the week, we had a wing chapel that would start to tear off my mask. We sat down on our bunks and Chaz told us the story of the Black Knight and how he never let anyone see what was under the armor. He told us that sometimes we hide what we are, and that we need to take off that armor. I realized that black knight was me. After that, he told us his story and it sent shock waves though me (I'm not going to tell you what his story was, but it was very similar to mine). Every chapel, Daniel said that if anyone needed to talk about something, all the leaders were ready to listen. The night after the Black Knight wing chapel, I stayed behind after chapel, found Chaz and started crying while telling all what had happened in my life. He cried with me and we talked for at least a half an hour before heading back to our cabin. We got back and that night was the night where we told our stories (which was totally a God thing). Chaz told his, then Jordan told his, then finally

BEST COUNSELOR Chaz spent extra with me because he saw me hurting.

I decided to tell mine. In the middle of my story, Austin got up and hugged me, then Daniel, then a line formed of my cabin mates who wanted to give me a hug. We finished the rest of the stories, and Tyler pointed out that all our stories were extremely similar!

It wasn't just me! I wasn't alone! It was at that moment, that my mask fell off. We all cried that night for each other. We became brothers. I had a new family.

After solving the world's problems, my week at GenJ came to an end. My brothers and sisters exchanged contact information and then

BROTHERS FROM A DIFFERENT MOTHER

we left for our homes in different states. Even though my mask was finally off, I still struggled with a lot of depression and anger at home. A couple months after I got home from camp, I got into a big fight with my dad at dinner and stormed off to my room.

I went back thinking that I was a nuisance and almost took my own life one last time. However, as I was on the floor sobbing and screaming at myself, God reminded me of all of the new family members from camp and my parents who loved me. I laid down on the floor and started crying even more because of all of the people who loved me. After at least 30 minutes, I looked up on my desk and saw my Bible, and remembered how happy my parents still were even though my dad had cancer. What if I was doing life all wrong? My parents prayed, they trusted God, and read the Bible while I wasn't doing any of that. I opened my Bible and turned to the book of Psalms (because I heard that Psalms is a great book to get peace) and started reading. I started to cry again because I realized that God didn't want to hurt me by going through this crazy adventure and throwing everything he could at me like I thought; He wanted to make me stronger and help me grow. I asked for forgiveness and became much happier.

Every year since my first GenJ I have gone back for spiritual healing and to see my family again. I didn't tell my mom my story until after my second GenJ camp and she was really happy for me. I didn't tell my dad until after my third GenJ, but ever since I told him, he and I have grown together and the fights have been very less frequent. I've been trying to fix my relationship with my brother, and we have improved a lot (Thank you Lord). I am so thankful that they never stopped loving me, but kept praying for me.

I've become much happier and feel better. Every once in a while, I do have days where depression rears its ugly head and I feel alone, but thankfully, it doesn't last long and I can fight it with truth.

At GenJ 2017, my mentor Jeremiah said since GenJ 2014, the staff had prayed for me and they were happy to see me smile again.

A couple days ago, my mom told me that right before my dad had his first surgery, they asked friends and family to pray for Zac and me to be drawn closer to God through these scary times and not be pushed away. Their prayers were answered in the most amazing way possible. I am thankful that I did go through these times and I thank God that he did put me through that time. If it wasn't for that time, I would not be the same man I am today.

Zac's Story

The worst year of my life started on the day everything seemed right.

The whole day I was hanging out with my best friend Matt at the old red park outside my house. It was a small rundown park. The slide was so loose it was almost falling off, the paint was chipped off, and you always had to avoid the occasional rusty spike sticking off of it; but we loved that park anyway because it was perfect for groundies. We would play groundies all the time

PARTY IN THE PARK Zachary and Matthew; best friends

to avoid work or get away from life. Matt was really good at it because he was a very skinny and small person at the time, so it was always impossible to find him. That day seemed almost perfect. It was nice and cool so we didn't have to worry about getting overheated or worry about getting too much water. It was perfect.

But like all good times it eventually had to end. Matt had to go home so I went back to my house too. Some part of me wishes I didn't but this would've been inevitable no matter if I went home or not. I opened my door and a blast of air conditioning hit me in the face and all was peaceful. I walked upstairs to my room

and laid down on my bed and started enjoying some music,
while I heard my brother playing with his Legos in his room.

Life was good … until it all of a sudden wasn't.

I heard my mom call me and my brother to come downstairs.
My brother and I raced down the stairs like we always did,
pushing past each other to grab the finial at the end of the banister
to swing faster down the stairs. When we made it to the bottom
we were met with the almost defeated faces of our parents.
They didn't want to tell us what had happened but they knew they
had to. They told us to sit down on what we called the "two couch,"
named cleverly by us because it could sit two people. Usually the
two couch was one of my favorites because it was so squishy
you would sink into it, but with the look I saw on my parents' faces
I couldn't enjoy it. Butterflies were fluttering in my stomach
as I waited for what seemed like hours to find out what my parents
deemed too hard to tell us.

When my brother and I were comfortable, my mom let us know that
my dad's brain cancer had come back. Now my brother and I had
done this once before, and it was bad the first time … the first time
around the cancer was stage 2 and it took all movement away from

my dad's right leg making him only able to walk with a sort of limp. This destroyed me because I loved playing soccer with my dad. One of my favorite things to do just ripped out of my life because of some stupid disease, never to come back. So you might be able to feel how far my stomach sunk after my mom told me it came back, but this time as stage 4 cancer (we later found out).

I was only eleven at the time but I wasn't an idiot. I could piece together that this was gonna take not just another leg, but take my whole dad. I was thrown into a state of depression that still hasn't totally gone away. It felt like I was thrown in a pit with no escape

SOCCER My dad loved watching me play. Before first surgery.

QUIET TIME WITH DAD Visiting my Dad after his second surgery

so I just had to sit there and suffer. It felt like time was moving around me but I wasn't able to participate. I bottled up these emotions and used comedy as a face I could put on to hide the fact I constantly wanted to die.

When my dad finally got put in the hospital, my brother and I were stuck at home. We couldn't visit him until after the surgery was over. It felt like years went by before we could go visit him. It felt like my life was a movie, only going through the motions, and not being able to change or affect the outcome. My friends would try to get my mind off of things but it would never work because of that little

HELPING KEEP MY MIND OFF THINGS Cousins Justin and Vanessa took us on many hikes

voice in the back of my head whispering, "Your dad is gonna die." I also tried to ignore life by locking myself in my room playing video games, but that would always be interrupted by someone knocking on our door giving us a casserole. Those casseroles would snap me back into reality. Snap me back to our sad life.

Finally the surgery was over and we were able to visit him. Hospitals have a certain smell to them. I hate it. I can't exactly describe the smell because it's so unique I can't relate it to anything. Nowadays whenever I walk into a hospital I want to throw up from that gut wrenching smell. My brother and I walked into his hospital room.

It was a big hospital room because my dad got so many visitors he needed more space. Two of the four walls were totally windows and one of them had a fantastic view of the mountains. You could get lost in their beauty and forget about life forever. When we walked in we saw him lying there so weak he could barely move.

"I'm so sorry buddy, but Dad will never walk again," my mom told me.

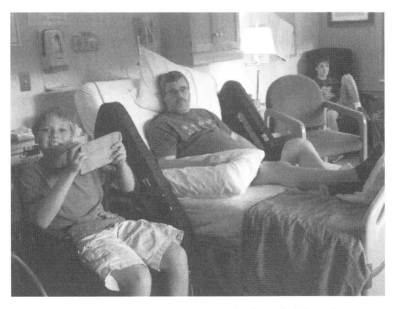

VISITING DAD Huge room, large windows with a view, a wall outlet . . . I'm in heaven!

I stormed out of the room and sat in the bathroom to cry. I had no idea how to process any of the information that I was just given.
I couldn't imagine what this was doing to him. Being stripped of his ability to walk after years of snow boarding, water skiing, and soccer must've killed him a hundred times more than it killed me.
Minutes felt like they turned into hours as I sat in the bathroom.
I finally came out puffy eyed and wet from tears.

After about a month he was finally able to come home. My brother and I made enormous welcome home signs that we hung from our

TAE KWON DO Keeping my attitude in check

DAD'S HOME He looked so weak

garage door. When he got home we could tell he loved the signs but we could also see his heart wasn't fully in it. My mom told us that he really did love the posters, but chemo left him so tired he couldn't fully express his emotions. To this day he still has to take his scheduled nap to recharge.

After months of physical therapy my dad was able to regain his ability to walk, or hobble that is, which scared the crap out of his doctor. "It's … not possible … I cut that part out of your brain!" exclaimed his doctor. "It's a miracle."

FEELING NORMAL Dad plus big chair equals good day

It wasn't long after that our parents told us we were moving to a one story house. I knew it was coming, it hurt, but after the past several months I had, it was nothing. I would never race my brother down the stairs again, never run down the street to hangout with Matt again, never see the mountains from my west facing window in my room, but none of it seemed to matter to me. My emotions were long gone to care anymore.

Years passed, and our new house was very cozy. A few years later my dad and I took a trip to California for him to work and for me to watch and learn how a graphic designer works in the real world.

I learned quite a lot on that trip including something that I never really thought would happen. We went out to coffee with one of my dad's old friends and that's when he told us that he was writing this book! My jaw hit the floor when he told me this. "You're writing a book?!"

My dad had never been good at reading or writing so I couldn't wrap my head around what he just told me. I pinched myself because it felt so out of the ordinary, it could only be in a dream. He went on to explain how the book was going to be about his fight with cancer and how no one should ever give up hope.

T-SHIRTS Dad's favorite work attire

I left that coffee shop with a little bit of a skip in my step. I truly felt like there was nothing on this planet that could keep my dad down. It helped me feel like there really was hope and that this disease wasn't just a road leading to the end. And above all else I felt truly blessed. I know the survival rates, I know the odds, and still my dad kept fighting back and he's still here today. But I know he has a huge hand helping him.

I don't know where you might put your trust, but I choose to put my trust in God. Only an all powerful loving Creator could keep my dad walking, working, providing, even after all that's happened.

PARIS Coffee with my dad at a Parisian Street Café

SUSHI It was great to experience Japan with Dad

To this day, I'll get hit with some unexpected tough times like every human. But I stay calm. Keeping my trust in the Creator keeps me calm. And I mean, what could be worse than what I've already gone through?

Caregiving by Kim

GBM Caregiver Thoughts

"We are all faced with a series of great opportunities brilliantly disguised as impossible situations." – Charles Swindoll

How do I navigate this with my kids?

"And all your sons will be taught of the Lord; and the well-being of your sons will be great." Isaiah 54:13 (NASB)

This is one of the biggies, so I'll start here. I won't lie or sugar coat; it has been rough at times. The Lord absolutely covered all of us through this, in spite of mistakes we made, and we are grateful. Our greatest desire through it all has been that it would bring Max and Zac closer to the Lord, and not push them away. We still pray that prayer.

Insist that they talk about everything; if not with you, then with a counselor who will keep pointing them to Jesus.

Have a support system in place just for them. Our kids had tremendous support from my parents, their youth pastor (Jake), and many other family members and friends.

Tell them as much as you can (gently, of course). Even though it's rough, they want to know. Otherwise, they will likely make up worse scenarios than the actual truth (even beyond the possible loss of their parent).

Reassure them that they will still be cared for, and it's ok to still be a kid. One of our boys was certain that he would have to quit school and get a job to help support us. We never, ever told him that; it was just in his nature to think he had to "man up." It broke my heart, and almost broke him.

Give your kids grace. Kids living in crisis or who have been through trauma need extra room to breathe and just "be." This doesn't mean excusing bad behavior; it's more about getting to the root issue.

Since we homeschooled at the time, this also meant going easy on academics when we were in the thick of the surgery and chemo days. They wouldn't have remembered what they studied anyway (same goes if they had been in a classroom)! Math was sometimes a game of Monopoly with Grandma, science was watching a Creation video with Grandpa, and PE was a hike in the hills with cousins Justin and Vanessa. Guess what? They caught up. Spending time nurturing their hearts was so much more important than worrying about long division.

As a former classroom teacher, I would add that it is critical to communicate with your child's teacher(s). Ask for lots of grace and modified assignments. Good teachers will be grateful to be in the loop.

Keep pointing out the places where God has been faithful.

Pray, and ask your friends to pray. It matters!

Shoutout to our kids — In spite of their struggles, they've both been an overwhelmingly kind and loving support for us, and we are crazy-blessed that they are our sons. They've had to grow up a lot quicker than we wanted, in many ways. But, they somehow knew how to rise to the occasion (even when "the occasion" was what we've come to call "awkward moments with dad," when they've had to do things like help him loop a belt, or pull him up from falling in interesting places …). Their love and thoughtfulness helped us all get through!

How do I handle this mentally/emotionally/spiritually?

"If you are not anchored in the goodness of God, you will lower your theology to match your pain." ~ Christa Black Gipporo

But He said to me, "My grace is sufficient for you, for my power is made perfect in weakness." 2 Corinthians 12:9 (NASB)

"When life is stormy, it is so easy to doubt … but I am learning that it is not the lack of storms in our lives that testifies of Jesus; it's the Savior in the boat." ~Unknown

Have you heard the quote, "Just because someone carries it well doesn't mean it's not heavy"? Yeah, that.

Caregivers often hear, "You're so strong! I could never do what you do! You're so inspiring!" I don't know about that.

No doubt, it feels good to be acknowledged, and to feel like I'm showing others it can be done. But it's definitely not "me." I've come to believe that the Lord gives us exactly what we need, when we need it — not too soon, and not too late. Look up the story of Corrie ten Boom's train ticket for a beautiful account that describes this thought more. But my point is, don't put yourself in my shoes and think you'd never make it. If you have Jesus, you will be ok when the time comes. I promise.

But the truth is, some days are harder than others, and GBM forever changed the course of our lives. It's something we live with daily. To be honest, it flat-out takes a commitment to have the courage to take every thought captive, and to live what you believe.

What does that look like?

Feel sad, discouraged, exhausted, weary, tired, angry, grumpy, cranky, annoyed … then acknowledging those feelings — even sitting with them a while — then consciously setting them to the side, taking a deep breath, telling myself to look for the good, and carrying on …

Say, "Thank you, Lord, for this hard or scary thing," even when I don't know the *why* or see the solution …

Consciously tell myself to think of the verses that apply in the moment. I used to write them out on 3"x 5" cards and tape them to my mirror or kitchen cabinets. These days I find pretty images on Pinterest and either print them out or keep them in a personal file for when I'm feeling down. Before one surgery I taped several in my hospital notebook. (Side note — Now is the time to tuck those verses away, so you have them when you need them later! Your mind will be mush; you'll just need them at your fingertips.)

Put a smile on my face and muster up a kind tone of voice, even when I don't feel it. The old "fake it 'til you make it" can actually help! Putting myself in his shoes helps too.

Stay faithful! Joseph had no idea if he would ever leave the prison. Neither did Corrie ten Boom. They just stayed faithful where they were, even when they didn't know the rest of their story.

Watch for the bigger purpose! Don't be afraid to be happy.
"In time of trouble say:

– First, God brought me here. It is by His will I am in this [hard] place. In that I will rest.

– Next, He will keep me in His love and give me the grace in this trial to behave as His child.

- Then, He will make the trial a blessing, teaching me lessons He intends for me to learn, and working in me the grace He means to bestow.

- Last, in His good time, He can bring me out again — how and when He knows." ~ Andrew Murray

"When I understand that everything happening to me is to make me more Christlike, it resolves a great deal of anxiety." ~ A.W. Tozer

How do I handle this physically and in a practical sense?

I had to pull back from all the commitments I used to enjoy. I realized that — shocker — I'm not Super Woman. I can only do so much, and I have to be mindful of that, and careful about how many things I put on my calendar. I used to "do all the things," but I just can't anymore. In some ways, it's disappointing; but in other ways, it's just a relief. It's self care, which is incredibly important to the marathon we're running. Self care is not selfish.

When people want to help you, let them. It does as much for them as it does for you. Our journey was eased tremendously by the amazing support we received along the way. The thoughtfulness and caring of family and friends made all the difference. Special thanks to my parents, whose thoughtful and practical help was invaluable.

Caregiving for Caregivers. Instead of saying, "Let me know if you need anything," try being specific. For example, ask, "When would be a good time for me to _____?" Or gift cards are always appreciated! Ideas include creating a meal train, grocery shopping, giving rides (appointments, kids' activities), picking up prescriptions, laundry, house cleaning, yard work, car care, pet care, short-term care for patient or children, computer/technical help, general errands (library, post office, etc.), or simple home projects. And never underestimate the tremendous value of sending a simple "I'm thinking of you" text, or just a listening ear.

Join a support group. I'm in a few on Facebook. These can be overwhelming, but the benefits of sharing the journey (usually) are worth it. We have made dear friends along the way.

Do all the "self care tips" the Internet tells you to do. I won't even write a list, because they're all pretty much the same. But, they can help. Or make up your own list; whatever works for you! My main thought here is that it's really true that "you can't pour from an empty cup." Don't feel guilty for taking care of yourself (I know, easier said than done).

What are some practical tips about the health side of things?

A Word about Doctors …

Our doctors' lack of specific knowledge about GBM was startling (remember it's a rare cancer). But even that became a blessing as we then felt the freedom to do our own research and carve our own path.

No matter how good your doctor is, you still have to advocate for your loved one.

These days, most doctors are open to what they call "adjunct therapy." In other words, they don't mind if you want to try a healthy diet or supplements, but they want to be seen as the first line of attack. And they want to be in the loop. I found that odd, since they typically shrug at anything natural. If that's the case, why worry about what they take? But clearly there is something to the natural route. It does do *something* in the body. So they want to be up to speed. That being said, I would listen to their advice, and then do my own research, pray, and proceed.

Examples:

I took Mark off of Essiac Tea for a couple of weeks before surgery. There is the possibility that one of the ingredients can be a (mild) blood thinner, which could have caused complications during surgery.

We were told "no vitamins" during chemo and radiation. Um, what? We wanted his body to be as healthy as possible to be able to fight! Anything that could be considered anti-inflammatory was a no-no. Again, what? We made the judgment call to (quietly) have him keep taking all the supplements recommended by our nutritionist. We definitely believe it helped him get through the treatment. And considering he is a long-term survivor, it clearly didn't hurt.

Speaking of supplements, here is a short list of some of what Mark has taken: Essiac tea, melatonin, fish oil, green tea, berberine, curcumin, multi-vitamin, isoflavone, Resveratrol and Nutriferon (Shaklee). He also takes Ritalin for energy and focus. This is not for all GBM patients, but has worked well for him.

We were given guidance about which supplements to take (and how much of each) by Nutritional Solutions (nutritional-solutions.net/). They fine-tune their suggestions based on each person's specific type of cancer and personal blood work.

They were also extremely helpful in addressing Mark's food aversions caused by treatment. We are forever grateful for family and friends who introduced us to Nutritional Solutions and who arranged for the cost of Mark's supplements to be covered.

Some legal stuff:

Get your wills, durable power of attorney, healthcare power of attorney, and trusts (if applicable) done NOW. Don't wait until you need it! There are ways to do this for free, but we recommend using a lawyer and having it drawn up specifically for your family. It can save headaches later.

Carry a copy of the healthcare power of attorney with you (if your loved one is ill). Give it to every new doctor or hospital you go to, and your health insurance company. They will thank you (and you will thank yourself later too).

Keep your HIPAA forms up to date. These may need to be updated every year!

Final thoughts...

A clear MRI is a relief! But it's short-lived relief, because we know it's just a snapshot telling us he's good up until this point. It does not guarantee anything at all for the future — not even the next 2 minutes! So we breathe a sigh of relief, but it's a weary sigh, not one of elation.

GBM is one of those relentless cancers that doesn't go into remission. Because Mark is a long term survivor, many people ask or assume he is in remission. But with GBM, that isn't a "thing." So we ask God to "keep on healing him," because that's the closest thing we can come to that describes our situation. It's healing that may or may not be temporary. It's a strange way to live, but perhaps good in its own way; living in the moment, and making the most of every opportunity. It's like we walk two parallel paths — one labeled "statistics," and the other labeled "but God." And really, as our attorney semi-joked, no one knows if or when they'll get hit by a Pepsi truck! Psalm 31:15 (NASB) says, "My times are in Your hands…" It's a comforting thought to hang on to.

I never would have chosen for my life (our lives) to look this way, but I am also thankful for what it has taught us and would never want to give that up. A friend who had cancer talked about it being a platform she had been given. Yes! In a very weird, upside down way, this has been a huge gift. We have "street cred" when we get to say, "God is faithful!" We try to take every opportunity we can to share Jesus, because that is our (not so secret) secret.

"We have this hope as an anchor for the soul, firm and secure." Hebrews 6:19 (NIV)

Resources:

Surviving Terminal Cancer by Dr. Ben Williams (a longterm survivor story)

The Musella Foundation for Brain Tumor Research & Information virtualtrials.com

(This includes valuable updates to the Ben Williams book, Surviving Terminal Cancer.)

Life's Mountains by Cheryl Broyles (Another longterm survivor. See also her website, cherylbroyles-gbm.com)

Hospitals known for their cutting edge research and treatment of GBM: Duke, M.D. Anderson, and Mayo Clinic. If possible, get a neuro-oncologist at "teaching hospital" on your team. They have access to the latest research and trials.

ClinicalTrials.gov Nutritional Solutions (nutritional-solutions.net) Targeted therapy for your specific illness.

The best anniversary ever!
Journal entry by Mark Almas 3/30/16

25 years ago, I married my best friend.
I committed to you, Kim, for better or for worse.
I am sure I've received the better. Kim you are
an amazing wife, friend, mother, and now
caregiver. I thank God for giving you to me.

I have loved every moment with you. Raising
two incredible sons with you (in spite of me)
has been a journey that has been awesome.
I love your love for traveling. Cruising
across the Atlantic, touring Europe,
are memories I'm not sure I would have
experienced, if not for you. You took me out of
my comfort zone. Working our way around our
own country, watching you homeschool Max
and Zac has been fun, and full of great
memories.

Kim, you are a rock! I can't imagine life without you. I am so glad to be here today to share our special day.

I am so thankful for all of you who have followed our journey, and have prayed us through. When you hear those words, "you have 12 to 16 months to live," you think through milestones you will miss. Sharing my 25th anniversary with Kim was at the top. I'm so glad God has allowed me this desire.

So here's to proving the doctors wrong another 25 years.

A couple weeks ago, we celebrated the life of a friend who lost his fight with ALS. I was reminded of the song below. A great song of love. I hope it touches your heart.

"I will be here"

Tomorrow morning if you wake up
And the sun does not appear
I . . . I will be here
If in the dark we lose sight of love
Hold my hand and have no fear
Cause I . . . I will be here

I will be here
When you feel like being quiet
When you need to speak your mind
I will listen
And I will be here
When the laughter turns to crying
Through the winning, losing and trying

We'll be together
Cause I will be here

Tomorrow morning if you wake up
And the future is unclear
I... I will be here
As sure as seasons are made for change
Our lifetimes are made for years
So I... I will be here

I will be here
You can cry on my shoulder
When the mirror tells us we're older
I will hold you
And I will be here

To watch you grow in beauty
And tell you all the things you are to me
I will be here, hmmm

I will be true to the promise I have made
To you and to the One who gave you to me
I will be here

And just as sure as seasons
are made for change
Our lifetimes are made for years

So I... I will be here
We'll be together
I will be here

Love ya, Babe!